American Politics:
A Beginner's Guide

"John Roper has long been one of the most astute foreign observers of the American political scene. This fine book promises a general introduction to its topic, but it delivers much more."

Cal Jillson – Professor of Political Science, Southern Methodist University, USA

"Excellent. Drawing upon his deep knowledge of American politics and history, and written with typical fluency, Roper has produced an eloquent supplement to general texts on American politics."

Chris Bailey – Professor of American Politics, Keele University, UK

"A lively and accessible text offering help to those entering the sometimes bewildering universe of US politics for the first time."

Niall Palmer – Lecturer in American Politics, Brunel University, and Associate Fellow of the Institute for the Study of the Americas, UK

ONEWORLD BEGINNER'S GUIDES combine an original, inventive, and engaging approach with expert analysis on subjects ranging from art and history to religion and politics, and everything in between. Innovative and affordable, books in the series are perfect for anyone curious about the way the world works and the big ideas of our time.

Beginners
GUIDES

American Politics
A Beginner's Guide

Jon Roper

ONEWORLD

OXFORD

A Oneworld Book

Published by Oneworld Publications 2011

Copyright © Jon Roper 2011

ISBN 978-1-85168-817-3

Typeset by Glyph International
Cover design by vaguelymemorable.com
Printed and bound in Great Britain by
TJ International Ltd, Padstow, Cornwall

Oneworld Publications
185 Banbury Road, Oxford, OX2 7AR, England

For Caitlin, Aisling and Jack

Contents

Acknowledgments

I first visited the United States as a graduate student. Jimmy Carter was President. I have been going back ever since. I would like to thank all those – friends, family and colleagues there – who have shown me such generous hospitality over the years. Through countless conversations I have learnt much about America from: Don and Beverly Davis, Bill and Anne Ehrhart, Gary Faulkner and Diane Levy, Sylvia Gaudlap, Fred Greenstein, Jack Godwin, Brad Henry, Trevor Nelson, Bill Nutter and Joni Bullard, John Pearson, Jim and Deb Pfiffner, Paul and Margaret Pinckney, Rick Sutton, and Susan Willey.

American Studies at Swansea University has been my academic home in the UK and I have been fortunate to work there with, among others, David Bewley-Taylor and Phil Melling. They have given generously of their time in discussing with me some of the themes explored in this book.

I have also benefited from the insights of Nigel Bowles, Phil Davies, John Dumbrell, Mike Foley, Timothy Lynch, Iwan Morgan, Bob McKeever and Ian Scott into American political ideas, institutions, society and culture. At Oneworld Publications, Mike Harpley commissioned the book and has seen it through to completion professionally and with good humor.

This book is dedicated to Caitlin, Aisling and Jack. To them, and above all to Nicola, thanks and love.

Introduction: Politics USA

American politics is exciting. It is compelling because of what the United States is and what it represents. America is the most powerful nation on the planet. Its industries and innovations drive the global economy. Backed by an arsenal of nuclear weapons, its military presence is felt worldwide. Countless Hollywood productions project its popular culture abroad. Throughout its history, the United States has been a magnet drawing immigrants from everywhere. They are attracted by what it offers: economic opportunities, political freedoms and the prospect of a better life. Americans participate in what Abraham Lincoln famously called "government of the people, by the people, for the people." Debates are heated. Freedom of speech encourages open discussion. Arguments can be highly charged as ideological opponents seek to sway public opinion on controversial political, economic and social issues. Politics in America matters.

It began as an experiment. At the end of the eighteenth century thirteen rebellious American colonies fought a war and won their independence from the British Empire. Their collective Declaration of Independence, issued on July 4, 1776, based its reasoning upon a democratic belief in an individual's equal rights to "life, liberty and the pursuit of happiness." Americans rejected the idea that those who inherited their position in society through an accident of birth should exercise political power.

Instead, they placed their faith in written constitutions that established new and more representative systems of government. In 1787 delegates from the independent states gathered in Philadelphia and ventured into unknown territory. They agreed a constitution that created a new nation: the United States of America. Nobody could safely predict whether or not it would endure.

With the outbreak of the French revolution in 1789, the year after George Washington had been inaugurated as the first President of the United States, it seemed that monarchies were on the retreat on both sides of the Atlantic. In 1804, however, after years of political turbulence, Napoleon Bonaparte became Emperor of France, extinguishing hopes of maintaining a republican government there. That same year, President Thomas Jefferson successfully ran for a second term. When Jefferson had entered the White House in 1800, following the election in which he defeated Washington's successor, John Adams, it marked the first time that executive power had been peacefully transferred from one political party to another. Whereas a fragile French democracy failed to find its foothold, America's federal republican government survived – despite the tragedy of the Civil War (1861–1865) which finally ended slavery in its southern states.

The issue of race remained a sensitive sub-text in the nation's politics. In July 2008 at a campaign event in Springfield, Missouri, Barack Obama, the first African-American to be nominated as a presidential candidate, made the prediction that at some point during the election that year the Republican party would try a scare tactic by suggesting that he did not "look like all those other Presidents on the dollar bills." He had made similar remarks previously elsewhere. This time his comment caused a flurry of accusations and denials that he had "played the race card." The brief but intense controversy highlights the cultural and historical baggage that accompanied his candidacy. For an

African-American to occupy the White House is undeniably an historic achievement. Obama is representative of a twenty-first-century American society that is becoming increasingly multi-ethnic and multicultural. After the election, President George W. Bush, in accepting his party's defeat, acknowledged the wider significance of Barack Obama's victory and "the strides we have made toward a more perfect union."

The struggle to advance the cause of democracy has defined American political life. The right to vote in elections was restricted initially by wealth, by gender and by race. By 1840, however, most of the white male population could participate in elections. The battle for the right of women to vote was finally won in 1920 with the passage of the nineteenth amendment to the Constitution. Yet it was only in the 1960s that the descendants of those brought to America as slaves could claim their civil rights and take part in national politics.

When decisions are made, it is the majority that rules. This simple political fact is both democracy's strength and its potential weakness. In his first inaugural address as President, Thomas Jefferson acknowledged that "though the will of the majority is in all cases to prevail, that will, to be rightful, must be reasonable." Similarly, James Madison, the architect of the Constitution and Jefferson's successor in the White House, realized that "If a majority be united by a common interest, the rights of the minority will be insecure." Democracy in America endorsed the strength of collective action when it was agreed by a majority of its citizens. Yet it was also recognized that minorities should still have the right to voice their opinions and squabble on the side-lines of national political life.

Jefferson, Madison and their contemporaries believed that in federalism – the coexistence of state and national governments – they had found a way of limiting the capacity for majorities to ride roughshod over minority opinion. Madison was convinced that American society would "be broken into so many parts, interests and classes of citizens, that the rights of individuals, or of the minority, will be in little danger from interested combinations of the majority." It followed from this argument that the more states that joined the union, the more pluralist its free-wheeling society would become. A belief in the advantages of federalism imparted an expansionist dynamic to the nation that led to forty-eight contiguous states eventually being carved out of the North American continent. An additional two – Alaska and Hawaii – also joined the United States, despite their geographical disconnection from it. Federalism continues to shape the landscape of American politics. Nowadays the distinctive traditions and individual concerns of the fifty states help to create a vibrant political culture that would have met with Madison's approval.

European monarchs had derived their legitimacy and authority from the idea of their "divine right" to rule over their subjects. They considered themselves accountable to God alone. Republican governments were answerable instead to their citizens. Separation of church and state lies at the heart of American political and constitutional thought. The first amendment to the Constitution prevents Congress from passing laws "respecting an establishment of religion" and "prohibiting the free exercise" of any faith. Yet this is not to deny the significant influence that religion has in shaping America's political culture. Faith remains important to many of its citizens, underpinning the contemporary moral climate and influencing attitudes toward political issues.

The democratic idealism that has defined the nation to itself has also shaped its sense of place in world affairs. Throughout the nineteenth century, the United States looked inward as it expanded across the North American continent. Nevertheless, the advance of democracy elsewhere in the world was seen as an endorsement of the way in which America had designed its system of government. John Quincy Adams, who in 1824 followed in his father's footsteps to become President, argued that the United States:

> goes not abroad, in search of monsters to destroy. She is the well-wisher to the freedom and independence of all. She is the champion and vindicator only of her own … She well knows that by once enlisting under other banners than her own, were they even the banners of foreign independence, she would involve herself beyond the power of extrication, in all the wars of interest and intrigue, of individual avarice, envy, and ambition, which assume the colors and usurp the standard of freedom.

Times change. During the twentieth century and beyond, as it has developed into an undisputed world "superpower," the United States has become more outward looking. It has seen its national security in terms of promoting the values of democracy abroad in order to preserve them at home. Moreover, America has shown itself prepared to exercise its military power overseas. Ignoring John Quincy Adams' advice, it has sent its troops abroad "in search of monsters to destroy" in both world wars, in Korea and in Vietnam during its Cold War confrontation with communism, and, in its response to the 9/11 terrorist attacks, in Afghanistan and Iraq. Belief that the United States now has a moral purpose – often expressed as a God-given providential mission – to advance the cause of democratic freedom throughout the world gives both direction and force to the formulation of foreign policy.

On December 1, 1862, with the nation he presided over fighting the Civil War, Abraham Lincoln sent his annual message to Congress. In it he famously described the United States as "the last best hope of earth." One month later, the President issued the Emancipation Proclamation, signaling the end of slavery should the Union win the war. It did. The United States survived the greatest threat to its existence. Almost one hundred and fifty years later, Barack Obama, an African-American from Lincoln's state of Illinois, felt empowered to run for and ultimately win what had until then been the white's house. His victory in the 2008 presidential election symbolized a potentially seismic shift in American politics. It pointed the way toward the nation's multicultural future, moving it beyond the long and bitter memories of its racially segregated past. Yet as the nation confronts fresh challenges in extending equality, liberty and the promise of American life to all its citizens, to fulfil the potential of a "more perfect union," its politics remain argumentative, inventive and brash. Democracy in America is still a fascinating work in progress.

1

Political foundations: "A republic if you can keep it"

Who wrote the documents that laid the political foundations of the United States of America and why do their words continue to inspire Americans? On July 4, 1776 the Declaration of Independence proclaimed that the thirteen British colonies clustered along America's Atlantic coastline no longer considered themselves part of the British Empire. It was an act of rebellion that inspired what Thomas Paine, the British radical who was a witness to the events, memorably called "a revolution in the principles and practice of government," transforming politics and international relations forever. In 1787, the Constitution created the United States as a federal republic and a representative democracy in which the government is accountable, through the ballot box, to the people. During the subsequent two centuries and beyond America would become, quite simply, the most powerful and important country in the world. It would promote its democratic ideals beyond its borders as a means of preserving them at home, believing that if its values are shared across the globe, it will have fewer enemies abroad. As the events of 9/11 so graphically illustrated, others do not share that vision.

To understand politics in the United States today, it is still essential to appreciate the audacity of that remarkable constellation of talent – the military heroes, the philosophers and the politicians – who were present at the nation's creation. The first three Presidents of the United States, George Washington, John Adams and Thomas Jefferson, were among the most prominent rebels. Had America lost the War of Independence, they might be remembered only as martyrs for their cause. Instead, their achievements are still celebrated. So too are James Madison's contributions to the development of the nation, as the principle architect of its Constitution and the Bill of Rights and as its fourth President. What they helped to create then endures now. How did they do it?

The immediate political purpose of the Declaration of Independence was simply to invite international recognition for the justice of the American case in the colonists' fight against imperial control. At the same time, it injected the ongoing war between two Georges – Washington and the British King, George III – with a revolutionary impetus that would ultimately lead to the creation of the government of the United States. Adams consistently argued for the Declaration's necessity. Together with Jefferson, who drafted it, he saw that those who had rallied to their cause had to provide a philosophical justification for their action. The colonial rebellion could be elevated into a fight for broader political principles. Their transcendent "idea of America" is thus expressed eloquently and concisely in the Declaration's assertion of self-evident truths: "that all men are created equal, that they are endowed by their Creator with certain unalienable rights, that among these are life, liberty and the pursuit of happiness."

Jefferson argued that when one form of government infringes those rights, then it may legitimately be changed for another. That was America's situation, exemplified in the Declaration's detailed list of colonial grievances against the British King. It was also a powerful indictment of the whole idea of monarchy, demonstrating that Americans like Jefferson and Adams were already thinking beyond their immediate struggle to break away from the British Empire and were considering the new political arrangements that could be made in what they now regarded as self-governing states. There was no prospect of George III in Britain being replaced by King George Washington in America. The post-independence constitutions of the former colonies would be emphatically republican.

The newly independent states were also independent of each other. Would they mirror continental Europe as a collection of neighboring nation-states? If so, would the outcome be political rivalries between them? Events in the decade after the Declaration hinted that this might well be the case. The colonies had united to win the war against Britain and had met together in the Continental Congress. This had agreed the Articles of Confederation, finally ratified in 1781 and intended to set up a limited form of national government. They proved inadequate to the task of arbitrating between states which had competing interests and conflicting priorities. The threat of European powers – Britain and France – exploiting internal instability after the War of Independence came to an end in 1783 led American politicians, most prominent among them Alexander Hamilton and James Madison, to argue for the need to create a stronger central government that would unite the states.

CONTINENTAL CONGRESS

During the American Revolution, representatives from the colonies met in Philadelphia to coordinate the political and military campaigns for independence. After meeting for the first time in 1774 to show the depth of opposition across America to British Imperial rule, Congress reconvened the following year as war broke out, setting up the continental army commanded by George Washington. In 1776, it issued the Declaration of Independence.

ARTICLES OF CONFEDERATION

The Articles of Confederation, drawn up by the Continental Congress, were the first attempt to establish a national constitution. The Articles committed the states to a "firm league of friendship" with each other. However, the national government had no powers over taxation or interstate commerce, and was without the capacity to enforce its legislation. The Philadelphia Convention of 1787 was called in order to address these deficiencies, but ultimately decided instead to design a new Constitution that created the United States of America as a federal democratic republic.

In 1787, Adams and Jefferson were both still on diplomatic missions overseas, but George Washington was persuaded to re-enter the political arena as President of the Constitutional Convention that met in Philadelphia. During May that year, delegates from all but one of the thirteen American states – Rhode Island stayed away – started gathering there to discuss a framework for a new national government. Four months later, thirty-nine of the fifty-five who had joined in the debates in Independence Hall signed their names to the Constitution of the United States of America.

A republican constitution

The Convention's proceedings were kept deliberately confidential so that political differences that might threaten the success of the enterprise were not made public. So on September 18, 1787, when Elizabeth Powel – a prominent member of Philadelphia society who had regularly entertained delegates, including George Washington, during their summer stay in the city – met Benjamin Franklin who, at eighty-one, was the most venerable among those who had witnessed the events inside the Hall, she took the opportunity to ask him what had been achieved. Was the United States to be a monarchy or a republic? The Convention was over and he could be candid. They had agreed, he said, to a form of government which was "a republic if you can keep it."

Franklin's reply was deceptively simple. On the one hand, it was reassuring. The Convention had kept faith with Adams and Jefferson. There was no real desire to import the form of government that their generation had rejected back into American political life. On the other hand, there was an awareness that, in designing a republic in which citizens had a say in electing representatives to institutions which had the power to make and execute laws in their names, Americans were making another leap of faith of the kind that had inspired the Declaration of Independence. The sixteen delegates who refused to sign the American Constitution evidently were skeptical about the success of this new experiment and Franklin's remark suggests that although, along with the other thirty-eight who had been prepared to add their names to the document, he was more optimistic about what had been achieved, he too was fully aware of the challenges that lay ahead. The concern was understandable, because at Madison's urging the meeting in Philadelphia had agreed to a new approach to the creation of a viable republic. He was confident that it would overcome the instability caused by the alternation of different factions in government, the main political problem that had afflicted America since the colonies had become states. But no one was sure.

Madison believed that the task of the Convention was to "decide forever the fate of Republican government." By that he meant that its task would be not only to strengthen the union of the states in order to preserve their independence. It had also to find a solution to the political instability that seemed to be endemic across America at that time and which was potentially fatal to the whole idea of representative government. Historically, republican experiments had failed. Madison was among those classical scholars who knew that in the ancient world, the republics of Greece and Rome had eventually collapsed. More recent events might have reminded him that a little over a century earlier, the attempt to do without a monarchy in Britain – Oliver Cromwell's Puritan commonwealth – had proved to be a relatively short inter-regnum before the restoration. Contemporary events in revolutionary France would soon confirm how quickly republicanism could turn toward civic violence and political turmoil.

During the colonial era, the American experience with democratic government had been limited largely to those New England town meetings that had allowed concerned citizens a voice in local politics. This form of direct participation in decision making was self-evidently confined to small populations. During the War of Independence, Adams and Jefferson had argued the case for popular sovereignty. The new governments of the states that replaced the colonial regimes were based emphatically and universally on the principle of delegated authority. The people chose representatives empowered to make political decisions in the legislature where laws were proposed, debated and either rejected or passed. These law-makers were then held accountable for their actions through what became that most democratic of inventions: the ballot box.

It was this that caused the problem. Elections were based on a simple idea. The candidate with the most votes won. Within state legislatures, a similar procedural device was then employed: those laws that attracted the support of a majority of representatives were enacted. But what happened if a majority was elected to the legislature that proceeded to enact laws in its own interests? This rapidly became the problem that had bedeviled American state governments in the highly politicized post-independence period. Contemporaries – Madison among them – identified it as a disease: the emergence of factions which pursued their own political agendas rather than the common good.

Factional politics created an atmosphere of instability, particularly in those states, such as Virginia, New York and Pennsylvania, that had adopted the radical mantra widely quoted among the revolutionary generation that "Where annual election ends, tyranny begins." Suspicion that the default position of politicians was to abuse power meant that in many cases majority factions were routinely turned out of office after twelve months. When this happened, a rival political grouping gained control of the legislature but was then subject to the same electoral sanction. Laws passed became laws repealed. In such circumstances, many Americans doubted if republican government could survive. Indeed, it was this concern that led James Madison and others down the road to Philadelphia in 1787. Convinced of the need to refocus Americans on the Jeffersonian ideals that had inspired the move to independence, their mission was nothing less than to reconstruct the idea of republicanism into a workable form of representative government. As representatives gathered at the Convention, however, it became obvious that political compromises would be necessary to persuade states to sign up to a new Constitutional settlement that would create a federal government. Nowhere was this more apparent than in the dispute that arose over the continuing presence of slavery in the South.

Slavery, its existence, its abolition and its legacy, has been a defining issue in the nation's political life. In remarks he made at the Philadelphia Convention Madison observed that: "It seemed now to be pretty well understood that the real difference of interests lay, not between the large & small but between the N. & Southern States. The institution of slavery & its consequences formed the line of discrimination." It was a major concern in Philadelphia in 1787 and influenced the eventual framework of government that was agreed there. Ultimately it provoked the South to leave the Union after Abraham Lincoln's election to the presidency in 1860. The Civil War ensured its abolition and that the United States survived as a federal republic. But the residual racism that endured for a century and more after the South surrendered at Appomattox continued to haunt American society. Madison was both right and prescient.

Aware of the deep divide between states that maintained slavery and those that did not, at the Convention, the less populous southern states were concerned to preserve their minority political influence within the proposed structure that created the government of the United States. They insisted on the clause in the Constitution which allowed them to count their slave populations in determining the allocation of seats in the federal House of Representatives. Slaves were the "three fifths of all other Persons" who, along with the free citizens of each state, counted for the purposes of apportionment. So the South was initially over-represented in the Congress and, by extension, in the Electoral College that was established to elect the President.

In this sense, it is no accident that of the first six Presidents of the United States, four came from Virginia. Moreover, southern states also had political parity in the federal Senate, where each state was represented by two senators. Such compromises were made possible because of the agreement in Philadelphia that the United States government should be anchored to the principle of federalism, the division of sovereignty that allowed a boundary to be drawn between the centralizing authority of the national government and the preservation of individual states' autonomy over their internal political affairs. Like many borders, however, this one would be constantly patrolled and often disputed.

Federalism, the separation of powers and checks and balances

It was Madison who ensured his reputation as the driving force behind the shaping of the Constitution by keeping the most complete account of the Convention's proceedings. This account reveals the way that, throughout the debates, delegates combined an intelligent understanding of political philosophy with an intuitive grasp of political realities. Moreover, it shows that genuine negotiations took place as each state accepted the need to give up some political ground in order to promote the collective security that was the anticipated outcome of strengthening the national government. In essence, this was the idea of federalism. It is nowhere more evident than in the structure of Congress, the legislature that was designed as the centerpiece of the Constitution.

From the outset, Madison attempted to hijack the Convention's agenda. Instead of allowing it merely to adhere to its ostensible purpose – to discuss revisions to the existing Articles of Confederation – he ensured delegates started by considering a radical new design for a national government. One feature of the Madison-inspired Virginia plan was its proposal for a bi-cameral legislature, in which the two houses would be elected independently and according to different rules, but in both of which the states would have a number of representatives allocated according to their populations. Less populous states saw the immediate political disadvantages in becoming an outvoted minority. The New Jersey delegation countered with its own plan, exploiting the sense of unease that the Convention was overstepping its original mandate and proposing to keep the national legislature that existed under the Articles of Confederation: a single chamber in which each state had equal representation.

Two delegates from Connecticut, Roger Sherman and Oliver Ellsworth, helped to broker the eventual agreement. There would be two houses in the legislature. One of them, the House of Representatives, would be elected by the people and each state's representation would be determined proportionately by a census of its population. In the other, the Senate, each state would have equal representation, with members elected by the state legislatures. The principle of federalism was enshrined at the heart of the American Constitution. The "Connecticut Compromise" created the federal Congress in the form in which it has since remained: the House of Representatives and the Senate, each with a distinctive role and purpose in the framework of the nation's government and politics.

The principle of federalism also introduced the potential for the expansion of the United States across the North American continent. Madison was not alone in realizing that "the accidental lucky division of this Country into distinct states" had the equally fortunate outcome of allowing the United States to increase in size according to the federal principle. Additional states were carved from new territories rather than as a result of existing states annexing more land at the expense of others. Moreover, he was convinced that the creation of more states imparted a political dynamic to the republic, allowing a greater diversity of interests to be represented across the nation and avoiding the creation of a fixed permanent majority that would pursue its own interests at the expense of the public good.

Slavery proved him wrong. Its persistence in the South meant that the acquisition and organization of new territory remained a contentious political issue. As the United States acquired fresh land, slave-owning southerners argued that what they came to refer to as their "peculiar institution" should be allowed to spread, while a growing number of northern abolitionists refused to countenance the contamination of slavery entering new territories. Congress brokered compromises. Eventually, however, southern states, increasingly perceiving themselves powerless in the face of an intractable northern majority, took the decision to leave the Union. The collapse of Madison's republican ideal into the chasm of the Civil War was a result of the collision between different interpretations of federalism, the running political sore of slavery and the inexorable demands of expansionism.

Ultimately, the only way to keep the republic, as Abraham Lincoln realized, was to fight for it.

Those gathered in Independence Hall in Philadelphia in 1787 would not have imagined that future for the nation they were attempting to create. Nevertheless, they did have some insight into the way in which the Constitution could create a political framework within which the different functions of government might be accommodated to one another. Federalism was not the only political idea elevated to a constitutional principle. Equally important was the doctrine of a separation of powers. This principle had already established itself in the newly independent states. John Adams had observed that:

> a legislative, an executive and a judicial power comprehend the whole of what is meant and understood by government. It is by balancing each of these powers against the other two, that the efforts in human nature towards tyranny can alone be checked and restrained.

He had come to that conclusion, like many colonial American politicians, from his knowledge of classical political philosophy, his study of contemporary French political ideas and his experience of British rule.

The ancient Greeks, notably Plato and Aristotle, had argued that an ideal form of government would reflect what they saw as the natural divisions within society between those individuals whose claim to political power was based on their birth-right, the enlightened few who professed to govern in the best interests of everyone and the wider community who expected a say in determining who had the authority to govern in their name. This combination of monarchy (rule by one person), aristocracy (rule by a select elite) and democracy (rule by the people) recognized the existence of a hierarchical society based upon social classes and gave each of these elements a stake in the system of government.

In eighteenth-century Britain, the legal theorist William Blackstone thought that the monarch and Parliament had achieved such a political equilibrium. In his view, King George III, together with the hereditary aristocracy in the House of Lords and those who had seats in the House of Commons, each played a significant role in the nation's political life. Blackstone's works were widely read in Britain's American colonies. More influential still were the ideas of the French Baron Montesquieu. He had looked somewhat enviously at the contemporary British constitution from across the Channel and argued that it was possible to assign separate powers to these three distinct hierarchical elements of society. So the King could have executive power, the House of Commons legislative power, with the House of Lords combining its judicial power with a role in legislative oversight.

As colonial unrest at the perceived injustices associated with British imperial rule grew during the last half of the eighteenth century, Americans argued that Blackstone's portrait of British government had become blurred beyond recognition. In the Declaration of Independence, Jefferson's criticism of George III was that he had become a tyrant and had undermined the balance of power between the monarch and Parliament. Nevertheless, Montesquieu's analysis still retained its appeal for many American colonists. What Adams and his contemporaries extracted from it was the idea that a separation of powers could be based not on social classes but on government functions: the Legislature which passed the laws, the Executive which oversaw their operation and the Judiciary which arbitrated their constitutionality. When it was combined with the principle of federalism, therefore, this formulation of the concept of a separation of powers would become the animating spirit of the American Constitution.

Recognizing the need to separate the legislative, executive and judicial functions of government did not mean the creation of a system in which there would be no political interaction between them. On the contrary, as Adams had appreciated, the challenge of creating a government in which each institution could be held accountable for its actions lay in determining the balance of powers between them and allowing each to check the others. So the American Constitution outlines how Congress, the President and the Supreme Court should work together to restrain and verify the actions each is empowered to undertake.

The President can veto legislation passed by Congress, but the veto may be overturned. However, the Supreme Court can still declare a law to be unconstitutional. The Executive can appoint members of the Supreme Court and make treaties with foreign powers, but subject to Senate approval. Both Houses of Congress can initiate legislation but the final version of any law has to be agreed between them. The House of Representatives can build a case for the President's impeachment, but that case is then tried before the Senate with the Chief Justice of the Supreme Court presiding. These are a few examples of the ways in which the Constitution of the United States, in its intricate and ingenious design, creates a system of government of – in the apt phrase used by the political scientist Richard Neustadt – "separated institutions sharing powers."

Where powers are not clearly demarcated between institutions or indeed between the federal and state governments, the Constitution sets in motion a political dynamic in which their relationships are constantly being re-negotiated. Both Congress – notably the Senate – and the President have influence over the nation's foreign policy. This can and does lead to friction between them. Similarly, at least until the end of the Civil War, the struggle over whether to permit or prohibit slavery in new states which joined the Union meant that the borders between federal authority and state autonomy were constantly shifting as the nation expanded westwards.

The electoral system

Federalism, the separation of powers and checks and balances, became the foundation stones of the new national government, but just as important were the discussions in Philadelphia as to how its representative elements were to be chosen. It was a straightforward decision to apply the principle of direct election to the larger of the two legislative chambers. George Mason from Virginia called the federal House of Representatives "the grand depository of the democratic principle of the government. It was, so to speak, to be our House of Commons." His fellow delegates understood his reference to the lower chamber of the British Parliament. They appreciated, moreover, that the American House of Representatives should be held accountable through the ballot box, but how frequently? Those who advocated annual elections and those who argued for a longer period between them – three years was a suggestion – eventually split their differences and settled on a two-year term for members of the House. The detailed mechanics of the electoral process were left to individual states to decide and it took some time for a more or less uniform district based system to be adopted across the United States.

The House of Representatives remained the only directly elected element of the federal government until a constitutional amendment in 1913 provided for the Senate to be elected in the same way. Until then, the Constitution had provided for each state legislature to have the power to decide who was sent to the Senate. Senators were to hold office for six years, with a third chosen every two years. Between the two-year term for members of the House of Representatives and the six-year term for Senators was sandwiched the four years that the President held office. The method of electing the Executive was again different. The Electoral College became the most anonymous and least understood institution in American political life.

The existence of the Electoral College is the product of fear and compromise. Delegates to the Constitutional Convention agreed that they could trust the wisdom of their fellow Americans in selecting the President of the United States only to a certain point. They were afraid that a direct election for the Executive was a democratic step too far. So they devised the Electoral College: an institution that allowed for popular participation but combined it with the potential for political guidance from the power-brokers of the new republic.

THE ELECTORAL COLLEGE

The number of votes a state has in the Electoral College is based upon the total number of representatives it has in Congress. This in turn reflects shifts in population and any changes are determined after each decennial census. So in 2008, for example, California was the biggest prize. With fifty-three members of the House of Representatives and its two Senators, it had fifty-five Electoral College votes. On the other hand, seven states (Alaska, Delaware, Montana, North and South Dakota, Vermont and Wyoming), together with Washington DC itself, each had only the minimum possible number of three Electoral College votes. To become President in that year, either John McCain or Barack Obama had to win a majority in the Electoral College: 270 of the 538 available votes.

In the first two presidential elections, the Electoral College voted unanimously for George Washington. However, as political parties became established in the new American republic it became evident that the institution might require some fine tuning. It was originally envisaged that the candidate with most votes there would become President and the runner-up would serve as Vice-President. That worked well initially for the elections of George Washington and John Adams. In 1796, however, the Federalist party candidate, John Adams, won, but his closest challenger, the Democrat-Republican Thomas Jefferson, became Vice-President, much to their mutual regret.

Four years later, things became more complicated. In 1800, parties had become sufficiently organized to run a "ticket" for both executive positions. However, Jefferson's supporters failed to arrange for their vice-presidential candidate, Aaron Burr, to be the runner-up when the Electoral College votes were counted. The Federalists ensured that Adams received one more vote than his running-mate, Charles Pinckney. Jefferson and Burr beat their rivals but not each other. The Electoral College dead heat meant that the election was decided by the House of Representatives, where the Federalists were intent on making political life as difficult as possible for their rivals. After an exhausting round of thirty-six ballots, Jefferson finally emerged the winner. In December 1803, Congress approved the twelfth amendment to the constitution which was ratified in June 1804. The Electoral College contests for President and Vice-President were separated in time to avoid the risk of another debacle in the presidential election held later that year.

It was left to individual states to decide how they selected members of the Electoral College. In the early years, different systems were in use: state legislatures sometimes elected them, or, where more direct democratic involvement occurred, voting took place in districts or statewide elections. Apart from a few historical anomalies, however, since 1832, Electoral College votes have been pledged to candidates on the basis of a "winner take all" system whereby gaining a simple majority within each state is sufficient to gain all that state's Electoral College votes. In the 2008 election, Obama had a comfortable margin of victory in California and with sixty-one percent of the popular vote won all fifty-five of the state's Electoral College votes. The race was much tighter in Florida but Obama still won all twenty-seven Electoral College votes there despite having a bare fifty-one percent of the popular vote. In North Carolina, with a third party candidate also gaining some support, the margin was even closer: John McCain was less than a percentage point behind in the popular vote but still lost all fifteen Electoral College votes to his opponent.

The Electoral College has from time to time produced controversial political outcomes. One problem that has recurred is that popular votes cast do not directly correlate to Electoral College votes won. That means it is possible for a candidate to win the popular vote and fail to gain a victory in the Electoral College. It happened most recently in the 2000 contest. According to the official Federal Election Commission summary of the results, the Democrat's candidate, Al Gore, had 50,999,897 votes, more support than the 50,456,002 who voted for the Republican George W. Bush. Yet when the Supreme Court ordered the recounting of disputed votes in Florida to stop, effectively awarding that state's twenty-five Electoral College votes to Bush, it was sufficient to give him a majority there of 271 to 266 and the keys to the White House.

A similar outcome had occurred three times previously. In the presidential election of 1824, none of the crowded field of four candidates gained an outright majority in the Electoral College. As had been the case in 1800, the election was then decided in the House of Representatives. Henry Clay was Speaker of the House. His fourth place in the race for the White House had removed him from contention. When Clay's supporters in Congress voted for John Quincy Adams rather than Andrew Jackson, and Clay himself became Secretary of State in the new administration, Jackson was convinced that a "corrupt bargain" had been struck. He had won the popular vote, but now saw the former President's son, whom he had defeated at the polls, become President in political circumstances that were as controversial as those which had ejected John Adams from the White House twenty-four years previously.

In 1876, Samuel Tilden, the Democrat candidate, won the popular vote. However, having initially failed to gain an outright majority in the Electoral College, Tilden was denied the White House after an electoral commission awarded twenty disputed Electoral College votes in Florida, Louisiana and South Carolina – former Confederate states still occupied by the Union army – to his Republican opponent, Rutherford B. Hayes. Amidst rumors of a political deal, President Hayes ended the military control of the South, effectively halting the process of Reconstruction there. Twelve years later, the incumbent President, Grover Cleveland, lost his first bid for re-election in 1888, despite winning the popular vote. His failure to carry his home state of New York as well as other key battleground states such as Pennsylvania and Ohio meant that the Republican candidate, William Henry Harrison, gained a majority of the Electoral College votes. In 1892, Cleveland re-captured the White House from Harrison, becoming the only President to serve two non-consecutive terms.

The Electoral College was just one part of the constitutional plan agreed by the delegates at the Philadelphia Convention in 1787. It was a fresh blue-print for what, at the time, was a radical proposal to create a republican democracy based upon the principle of representative government. It was an experiment and no one knew with certainty whether it would be a success, or indeed if it would outlast their lifetimes. Over the next two centuries, changes would be made, fresh compromises agreed and the strengths as well as the weaknesses of their achievement would be exposed. But as Ben Franklin emerged onto the city's streets, like other delegates, his concern was more immediate: would his fellow Americans agree to ratify the plan?

Ratification

The Constitution was written in order to change the prevailing political culture in America. The states had fought successfully for their independence from Britain. Nevertheless amid the euphoria of victory there persisted a residual resentment among many former colonists at what they had regarded as the oppressive tyranny shown toward them by the British government. This made them instinctively reluctant to support the idea of a new federal authority – even if it was their own creation – now imposing laws on them. Constitutional ratification therefore became a political challenge. Indeed, if some of the larger states refused to approve the document, then the idea of creating the United States of America might have been short-lived. The Constitution's supporters went onto the political offensive. It was New York in particular, a key barometer of public opinion, where those who had been party to the secret discussions in Philadelphia sought to justify the outcome of their deliberations.

James Madison and Alexander Hamilton, along with John Jay, a former President of the Continental Congress, writing together under the generic pseudonym *Publius*, contributed a series of eighty-five articles to a New York newspaper which were subsequently collected and re-printed in book form as *The Federalist*. Madison and Hamilton had debated the Constitution at the Convention and Jay, although he had not been present in Philadelphia, was a long-time advocate for the need to create a stronger national government. They laid out the arguments in favor of union in an attempt to convince skeptical New Yorkers – and others elsewhere as *Publius* became a syndicated columnist in newspapers across America – that the government of the United States was a good idea.

Madison explained his constitutional design in his first and most celebrated contribution to the series. In *Federalist 10* he outlined how the federal structure of the United States would overcome factionalism: the political problem that had emerged in the newly independent states and which had historically caused republican governments to fail. Indeed, it had been "the instability, injustice and confusion introduced into the public councils" which had "been the mortal diseases under which popular governments have everywhere perished." Why was the affliction fatal? It was because of the procedural implications of majority rule. More often than not, when a self-interested majority faction controlled the government it was tempted to ignore abstract principles of justice and to threaten individual and minority rights. It was "the superior force of an interested and overbearing majority" that was the republican problem.

Madison argued that the American constitution would avoid this pitfall. He saw the United States as an extended republic that would prevent a fixed majority faction or party gaining and then abusing political power. Instead a multiplicity of interests would continually negotiate their conflicting agendas in a free-wheeling system that allowed them representation at both or either the state and federal levels. Critical to this vision was the dynamic of territorial expansion:

> extend the sphere, and you take in a greater variety of parties and interests; you make it less probable that a majority of the whole will have a common motive to invade the rights of other citizens; or if such a common motive exists, it will be more difficult for all who feel it to discover their own strength, and to act in unison with each other.

Madison thus argued that: "in the extent and proper structure of the Union, therefore, we behold a republican remedy for the diseases most incident to republican government." That was the hope. The reality was somewhat different.

It is one of the ironies of American politics that Madison's constitutional design has survived for over two hundred years despite its proving rarely fit for purpose. The principle of federalism was insufficiently flexible to accommodate the political tensions caused by the persistence of slavery in the American South. In turn these were exacerbated as the United States expanded rapidly across the continent in the early years of the nineteenth century. It was when southern states felt that they were, in the words of John C. Calhoun, the Senator from South Carolina, "a fixed and hopeless minority" that they triggered the secession crisis, claiming a right no longer to belong to the United States of America. The result of their action was Civil War. Its outcome – the Union victory over the Confederacy – preserved the principle of American federalism in a somewhat different form. The balance of political power within the federal system moved away from the states and decisively toward the government in Washington DC.

In the twentieth century and beyond, the increasing political spotlight on the federal government and its role in promoting economic stability and growth, as well as social, welfare and political reforms, together with the emergence of the United States as a world power, raised the issue as to whether the Constitution could still operate in the way Madison intended. In particular, the eighteenth-century framework of government has struggled to contain the apparently remorseless growth of presidential power in the twentieth century and beyond. The checks and balances in the political system which were designed to prevent any one institution of the federal government accumulating too much power have not always operated effectively.

Nevertheless, *The Federalist* still provides a unique and lasting insight into why those who supported the Constitution believed that federalism, the separation of powers and a system of checks and balances offered the best prospect for the survival of the republican ideal in America. Yet when New York became the eleventh state to vote in favor of ratification in July 1788, making the prospect of forming a government of the United States a political reality, it was not only because *Publius* had proven persuasive. It was also because its advocates had agreed to amend the constitutional design and add to it a Bill of Rights.

The Bill of Rights

In 1791 the first ten amendments, subsequently known as the Bill of Rights, were debated in Congress and added to the Constitution. Originally there were to have been twelve of them. However, the first two proposed amendments, specifying changes in the ratio of representatives to population as the numbers in the House grew and detailing the timing of any increments to congressional salaries, were not approved. In the final version of the Bill of Rights, therefore, it was the third congressional proposal that became celebrated as the first amendment to the Constitution, and not simply because of its eventual position in the list.

Its succinct language set an important tone, clearly defining the sphere of individual autonomy into which government should not intrude. In addition to preserving freedom of religious faith, it prevented any congressional legislation "abridging the freedom of speech, or of the press; or the right of the people peaceably to assemble, and to petition the government for a redress of grievances." The religious tolerance enshrined in the first amendment, together with the freedom of individuals and the media to express opinions, the right to hold public meetings and to ask the government to act if there is cause for complaint are nowadays regarded as vital signs of democratic life. Indeed, it is the first amendment that establishes basic standards for a functional republican democracy.

"A well regulated Militia, being necessary to the security of a free State, the right of the people to keep and bear Arms, shall not be infringed." If the first article of the Bill of Rights is justifiably famous, what follows in the second amendment is necessarily notorious, given the development of a gun culture in the United States which has elevated it to an article of faith. Read in its entirety it is a contingent right and its premise and purpose is plain. If America was to maintain the voluntary civilian organizations – such as the Minutemen of New England who had found fame during the War of Independence – that could act as a defense against potential internal or external threats to the security of the nation, then it made sense for them to be guaranteed the right to be armed. However, ignore its first thirteen words and the remainder of the amendment can be – and is – quoted as giving Americans a constitutional right to acquire and deploy the extensive personal arsenals of weaponry that nowadays have become an endemic feature among sections of national society.

Whereas the second amendment remains contentious, the third has become redundant. It protects citizens from having to give house room to soldiers either in peace-time, or in war-time unless prescribed to do so by law. The fourth amendment, protecting individuals against "unreasonable searches and seizure," limits the government's capacity for intrusive investigations without specific warrants defining their scope. It is followed by three further amendments which outline the procedures to be followed in cases of criminal prosecution and in common law suits. "Taking the fifth" has become a shorthand expression that invokes the individual's right to silence to avoid self-incrimination outlined in that amendment. The sixth amendment establishes the "right to a speedy and public trial, by an impartial jury," a precondition for the application of justice that is similarly endorsed in the seventh amendment in cases where the value of the dispute exceeds what is nowadays the meager amount of twenty dollars. The eighth article of the Bill of Rights, like the second amendment, has remained a source of political controversy. In specifying that "cruel and unusual punishments" should not be inflicted, it brings into the arena of public debate the continued use of the death penalty and the variety of methods American states have adopted to implement it.

Having outlined specific individual rights together with procedures for prosecutions and prescriptions for convictions, the final two amendments which make up the Bill of Rights are left deliberately vague. The ninth amendment points out that the rights included are not exhaustive: there are others that are equally legitimate and are "retained by the people." Finally, the tenth amendment once more endorses the principle of federalism by reserving any powers that are not constitutionally delegated to the federal government "to the States respectively, or to the people."

Federalism, separation of powers and checks and balances were constitutional devices that sought to hardwire systems to control the flow of power through the circuitry of national politics. However, the Bill of Rights went further still in its commitment to the idea that individuals should have constitutionally enshrined protections against the arbitrary use of government power. Some of its provisions are contentious, others may appear irrelevant to the twenty-first century, but it remains symbolically significant in shaping the political culture of America's republican democracy. It was a major contribution to the creation of the United States as a nation governed by the rule of law.

If the challenge of the Constitution often has been to make it work despite its inadequacies, it has survived because of its powerful role, alongside the Declaration of Independence and the Bill of Rights, in embedding the American idea of democracy at the heart of the nation's political culture. The democratic values of equality and liberty, expressed in the Declaration, endorsed in the Constitution and enshrined in the Bill of Rights, have been an aspiration for those initially excluded from full citizenship within the United States. They remain an inspiration for those in other countries who have successfully fought for them or continue to struggle for democratic reforms.

America was the first nation in the modern era to create a democratic republic. It was an experiment. As such, its outcomes were uncertain. The impact of republican democracy on the nation's political culture took time to assess, but as the institutions of the federal government became established, the United States became a laboratory of democracy which was under constant scrutiny, not least among Europeans curious to see how it developed. The most famous of these foreign observers was Alexis de Tocqueville, the French aristocrat who traveled to the United States in the 1830s to examine American democracy in action. His two-volume work, *Democracy in America*, remains one of the most trenchant analyses of how a dominant idea can shape the political culture of a society.

While Madison confidently believed that federalism and a separation of powers was a way of neutralizing the potential for a majority to shape the political life of the nation, the possibility that its influence might still be felt in other, more subtle ways could not be dismissed. This was Tocqueville's unique insight. He saw that in the cacophony of political voices echoing around Madison's pluralist republic there was one that drowned out the rest: the voice of the people. It was at its loudest when a majority expressed the same point of view. Tocqueville observed that: "in the United States the majority governs in the name of the people, as is the case in all countries in which the people are supreme." Moreover, even if the majority view was manifestly mistaken or absurd, it still carried the day because, as Tocqueville emphasized, "*there is no moral power above it*" in a society in which numbers always counted for more in any political argument. This, then, is a new form of democratic despotism, which Tocqueville called the "tyranny of the majority." It expressed itself not through victories at the ballot box nor in the state and federal Legislatures, but by influencing attitudes, opinions and political behavior.

Tocqueville saw the conformist pressures that built up within American society. In his travel journal he wrote of "the plane of uniform civilization" that had passed over American society. "The man you left in New York you find again in almost impenetrable solitudes: same clothes, same attitude, same language, same habits, same pleasures." His observation is an early example of a recurrent criticism of America's democratic culture. It may be populist but it is bland. Spreading across the continent during the nineteenth century, and then in the twentieth century overseas, "Americanization," for its critics, was a force to be resisted rather than imitated.

Despite Tocqueville's concerns, the Declaration of Independence, the Constitution and the Bill of Rights still symbolize a unique political achievement: the creation of the United States of America. In their separate but related ways, each was a product of the fear that power can corrupt and be abused. This conviction characterizes the nation's political culture. Americans fought to free themselves from what they perceived as the tyranny of the British King. They designed a Constitution in which power was intentionally diffused in order to constrain its use. The Bill of Rights was an attempt to define further the boundaries of governmental power in order to prevent it eroding individual autonomy. It established important legal processes that codified procedures for arrest, trial and sentencing.

Yet it was not the problem of power that became the greatest challenge to America's democratic republic, but rather the problem of the powerless. While the principles of equality and liberty coexisted with the reality of slavery in its southern states, the tensions within the United States were recurrent sources of political instability. The republic was kept only at the cost of the Civil War. It is the intermingling of these threads in the tapestry of the constitutional debate that took place in Philadelphia in 1787 – over power, slavery and the potential for expansion – and their subsequent historical combustion that provides an important context for an understanding of contemporary American politics. The United States often looks to the future by reminding itself of its past. Political speeches typically contain references to the events, ideas and aspirations of the founding period. Histories of that time and biographies of the principal actors in the drama of national creation remain both commonplace and popular. The values of the Declaration, the principles of the Constitution and the protections afforded by the Bill of Rights are the compass points of political debate. Ben Franklin's laconic remark to Elizabeth Powel still resonates. The past is indeed prologue and the United States remains "a republic, if you can keep it."

2

The federal government: "Separated institutions sharing powers"

When Edward Kennedy died in August 2009 he was widely eulogized as the "lion of the Senate." He had become the patriarch of one of America's foremost political clans after two of his elder brothers had been assassinated. Jack and Robert Kennedy were also Senators. One went on to become President, the other died while campaigning for the White House. After his own failed bid for the Democrats' presidential nomination in 1976, Ted Kennedy had remained the Senator from Massachusetts, a position he held for forty-seven years. In many ways, as his obituaries pointed out, he had been able to achieve more than either of his siblings, not simply because their lives had been cut tragically short, but because, unlike them, he had remained in Congress: the place where America's laws are made.

If the Executive is about political leadership, the Legislature is about political outcomes: it is where the business of American government can continue under the watchful eye of the Judiciary, acting as the guardian of the Constitution. The politics and the government in the United States intersect in the framing of laws, in the constantly shifting balance of power between institutions, in the perennial problem of presidential power and in the important area of judicial review. American government takes shape in an arena of constant negotiation and compromise between these "separated institutions sharing powers." The political process may at times seem messy, frustrating and unpredictable, but therein lies its fascination.

JUDICIAL REVIEW

The doctrine of judicial review is an American invention that has had a profound impact in defining the role of the Judiciary within the United States. The courts have the final say as to whether actions of the Legislature and the Executive conform with the legal framework set out in the Constitution and its subsequent amendments. The doctrine cements the Supreme Court at the core of the American political system through its power to interpret the Constitution and its commitment to upholding the principles of the rule of law and limited government.

Congress is unreliable. It doesn't always do what the President wants. Indeed, it is always possible and frequently the case that a Chief Executive is confronted by the opposition party controlling either the House of Representatives, or the Senate, or both. In the last fifty years, divided government has been the rule rather than the exception in Washington DC. Moreover, even if the President's party does predominate in both the House of Representatives and the Senate, there is no guarantee that the Legislature will enact the Executive's proposals. Party fortunes fluctuate. The entire House and one-third of the Senate face the electorate every two years and in Congress political perspectives and loyalties are shaped accordingly. Congress is a consistent complication each President must face because it is independently powerful, separately elected and fiercely protective of its constitutional position.

It is in the changing political dynamic between President and Congress that the constitutional principles of the separation of powers and checks and balances thus find their constant expression. James Madison and his contemporaries envisaged that Congress would have the central role in the nation's government, but they also ensured that it was not left entirely to its own devices. The Constitution makes it clear that "All legislative Powers herein granted shall be vested in a Congress of the United States, which shall consist of a Senate and House of Representatives" at the same time as it requires the President to "give to the Congress Information of the State of the Union, and recommend to their Consideration such Measures as he shall judge necessary and expedient." Nowadays, having become the focal point of the federal government, the President's task is to work with Congress to try to persuade it to support the Executive's political agenda. At the same time, the White House can also refuse to accept the laws which are passed on Capitol Hill.

The veto power

Every act Congress passes must be signed into law by the President before it can be enacted. The Constitution specifies that this should be done within a ten-day period (excepting Sundays). If the Executive disapproves of any measure, it is sent back to the Legislature. That is not the end of the matter. Congress can then reconsider and if a two-thirds majority approves, the law is enacted despite the President's veto. If Congress adjourns within the ten-day approval period, however, the White House has a political trick up its sleeve. A measure can fail to be enacted simply because it has been neither signed nor returned. Since much legislation tends finally to emerge from Congress under the pressure of an imminent vacation, the presidential "pocket veto" is another way of preventing a law reaching the statute books since it does not give the Legislature any opportunity to overturn the Executive's action.

"Pocket vetoes" can cause political controversy. In November 1983, President Reagan used the power to strike down a law that prevented military aid being given to El Salvador unless his administration could show that it had improved its record on human rights. However, Congress disputed his action, arguing that since law-makers had been merely between sessions, technically Reagan could not use the "pocket veto." Legal wrangling continued until the case finally reached the Supreme Court in 1987. The Court refused to make a definitive ruling. By that time, the original bill had expired and so it did not make much difference whether or not it had been passed into law. The Court neatly stepped through a political mine-field which might potentially have set it at odds with the other institutions of the federal government.

One way of assessing the health of the relationship between the Executive and the Legislature and who is in the political ascendancy is by seeing how much congressional legislation a President vetoes. In the early years of the Republic, the power was used sparingly: George Washington vetoed two measures and his five immediate successors exercised the option only a further eight times between them. Andrew Jackson, who was more aggressive in his assertion of presidential prerogatives, used his veto power on twelve occasions. Typically, however, presidential objections were infrequent. Moreover, the Legislature usually deferred to the Executive when laws were returned unsigned. Before the Civil War, Congress overturned just six of the fifty-two presidential vetoes.

After 1865, as Congress moved to re-assert itself following the period of national emergency when it had largely acquiesced to President Lincoln's leadership, his two immediate successors reacted by vetoing an unprecedented number of measures. Between them Andrew Johnson and Ulysses S. Grant refused to

approve legislation on 122 occasions. Johnson, who so antago-
nized Congress that he was eventually impeached, still holds the
record for the number of times – fifteen – that Congress
over-rode his objections. The potential for the White House and
Capitol Hill to be at loggerheads became an ever-present
political reality. In the late nineteenth century, in his two separate
terms in office, Grover Cleveland objected to 584 measures sent
to him by Congress and was, at the time, by far the most prolific
Chief Executive in his use of the presidential veto.

In the twentieth century, Presidents were typically more
prepared to defy Congress than were their nineteenth-century
predecessors (Cleveland apart): an indication of their increasing
involvement in shaping the nation's legislative agenda. Indeed,
while he was in the White House, Franklin Roosevelt used his
veto power as one way of reminding Congress as to who was
really in control of the national government. His message was
effective: only on nine out of the 635 times Roosevelt objected
to its legislation did Congress persist in enacting a law.

The veto power is potentially the final hurdle that has to be
negotiated before a law can be placed upon the statute books. It
represents the President's weapon of choice when faced with a
legislative initiative that the White House finds unacceptable. But
Congress too has a formidable arsenal at its disposal that it can
deploy to disrupt the Executive's efforts to enact its political
agenda. For a start, it has the power of the purse. The House of
Representatives approves the raising of taxes and between them
both Houses of Congress agree how it is to be spent. The
President's budget for the activities of the federal government has
to be approved by the Legislature, which can shape it, change it
or disapprove of it entirely. Moreover, law-making in America is
a tortuous process: procedural rules in Congress mean that
initiatives, whether they come from the Executive or from within
the Legislature itself, have to take their chances in the obstacle
race that has to be run before they can be enacted.

Congressional committees

If Congress is the most powerful independent Legislature in the world, its committees are the guardians of its prerogatives. They determine what is done, and more often what is not done. The committee system developed in the House of Representatives as a pragmatic response to America's population increase and as more states joined the Union, increasing its size. By the beginning of the twentieth century, Woodrow Wilson, then president of Princeton University rather than of the United States, summed up the problem and its solution:

> A numerous body like the House of Representatives is naturally and of course unfit for organic, creative action through debate … It organizes itself, therefore, into … standing committees permanently charged with its business and given every prerogative of suggestion and explanation, in order that each piece of legislative business may be systematically attended to by a body small enough to digest and perfect it.

Although the Senate is far smaller than the House, it too has developed its committee system. In both Houses of Congress committees are a natural organizational response to the issue of legislative efficiency. But they also shape the political landscape on Capitol Hill. Every aspect of their conduct is politicized: from who chairs them, who is assigned to them, to the legislative tasks they are given and how they perform their functions. They can be criticized on the one hand as products of patronage or powerful political fiefdoms and on the other as diverse outposts of political authority that undermine the capacity of the Legislature to act as a unified whole. Yet Congress cannot function without them. Wilson indeed observed that "the business of the House is what the committees choose to make it" and the same is true of the Senate. Of the thousands of bills and resolutions proposed each year, it is the committees which ultimately determine the legislation that Congress debates, passes and sends to the President for approval.

Once a bill has been proposed in either the House of Representatives or the Senate, it is allocated to a congressional committee for detailed consideration. This is typically a straightforward matter; for example, bills that involve taxation will automatically be referred to the Ways and Means Committee of the House or the Finance Committee of the Senate. However, the Speaker of the House and the Senate Majority Leader have the power to decide which committees they prefer to consider those legislative proposals when it is not automatically obvious as to where they should be allocated. That decision can dramatically increase or decrease a bill's chances of becoming law. Indeed, it will often be known in advance which committee will look favorably on a particular measure and so it is a political decision as to where they are sent. Nine out of ten bills stall at the committee stage, never emerging to be voted on by either the House or the Senate as a whole. The committee system creates an obstacle course for legislation. President Obama's healthcare proposals had to be negotiated through a number of congressional committees in both the House and the Senate, each of which could delay its progress, before the landmark legislation was finally agreed and passed into law.

Congress is not only a law-making institution. In its investigative role, it can turn the spotlight of scrutiny on areas of public concern. It also holds the Executive to account for its actions. Sometimes these two functions overlap. Although it was two indefatigable journalists – Bob Woodward and Carl Bernstein – writing for the *Washington Post* who unearthed Richard Nixon's conduct during the Watergate scandal, the President's political support in Congress was crucially undermined by the revelations brought to light in the hearings of the Senate Select Committee to Investigate Campaign Practices chaired by Sam Ervin.

Ironically, Nixon's political career had been given an initial boost as a newly elected member of the House of Representatives when he had been an investigator rather than the investigated. Assigned to the House Committee on Un-American Activities, he had pursued the case of Alger Hiss, who had served in Franklin Roosevelt's administration, and had eventually exposed him as a former member of the American Communist Party. It established him as a rising star in Republican politics. When he resigned rather than face the inevitability of a successful impeachment, Nixon may have reflected that congressional oversight can break as well as make political reputations.

Congressional investigations can also mold American political culture and public opinion. Joseph McCarthy used the Senate committee he chaired to foment the Cold War anti-communism of which the Hiss case had been a part. Before McCarthy's allegations and accusations were shown to be largely absurd, he had briefly convinced many Americans that communist infiltration of the government, the entertainment industry and other aspects of national life was a clear and present danger to the survival of the republic.

McCarthy stifled dissent through exploiting communal fear. A decade later, the Senate Foreign Relations Committee, chaired by William Fulbright, played an important role in allowing public misgivings to be expressed about America's war in Vietnam. In 2001, Committees in both Houses of Congress launched investigations into President Clinton's use of his power of pardon in the last days of his administration, particularly the case of Marc Rich, a fugitive from US justice whose wife had donated millions of dollars to the President and the Democrat party. More recently still, in November 2008, the Senate Armed Services Committee chaired by Senator Carl Levin published its inquiry into the treatment of detainees in US custody as a result of President George W. Bush's "war on terror." It concluded that in the aftermath of the attacks of September 11, 2001, "senior officials in the

United States government solicited information on how to use aggressive techniques, redefined the law to create the appearance of their legality, and authorized their use against detainees." As the Ervin, Fulbright and Levin Committees show, responsibly used, the power of congressional investigation is vital in maintaining public confidence in the nation's democratic institutions, monitoring the conduct of American government and holding its officials to account.

In addition to its legislative and investigative roles, the Senate also has an important part to play in ratifying treaties. Indeed, Woodrow Wilson should have known what he would be up against. In his series of lectures at Columbia University, subsequently published in 1908 (and still in print) as *Constitutional Government in the United States*, he argued that the Founders had intended:

> that the Senate would give the President its advice and consent in respect of appointments and treaties in the spirit of an executive council associated with him … rather than in the spirit of an independent branch of the government, jealous lest he should in the least particular attempt to govern its judgment or infringe upon its prerogatives.

Yet by the time Wilson entered the White House, jealously independent is precisely what the Senate had become. So it was that in his losing battle to persuade it to ratify the Treaty of Versailles, Wilson would not only destroy his health. He also failed to secure what might otherwise have become the crowning achievement of his administration. He suffered a massive stroke during a nationwide speaking tour intended to drum up public support for the treaty. The United States also refused membership of the League of Nations, Wilson's vision for a forum to resolve international conflict.

TREATY OF VERSAILLES AND THE LEAGUE OF NATIONS

The Treaty of Versailles concluded the First World War. President Wilson's major contribution to it was the proposal for a League of Nations to act as an international forum for conflict resolution. Isolationists in the Senate rejected the Treaty out of concern that American membership of the League would drag the United States into future wars. The Versailles Treaty imposed a punitive settlement on the defeated belligerents and without American participation the League proved ineffective. Within twenty-five years, a resurgent Germany precipitated another world war and American soldiers were once more fighting on the battlefields of Europe.

The Senate's rejection of the Treaty of Versailles remains an outstanding example of its power to influence United States foreign policy. It can also shape the contours of American domestic politics through its power to confirm or deny the President's nominees to the Supreme Court, to the Cabinet and to other senior positions within the federal government. Given the significance attached to appointments to the Supreme Court, the political stakes surrounding nomination and confirmation are often at their highest. During the last thirty years, on three occasions, the candidates chosen to fill vacancies have caused controversy. In 1987 the Senate rejected Robert Bork, a Reagan nominee. Two other candidates have subsequently withdrawn themselves from consideration rather than be subjected to congressional scrutiny. After Bork, Reagan's second choice, Douglas Ginsburg, requested not to be considered after facing allegations about his use of illicit drugs. In 2005 Harriet Miers, who had been nominated by George W. Bush, also withdrew after questions had been raised concerning her legal competence.

Even the prospect of hostile confirmation hearings in the Senate may thus be sufficient to discourage potential nominees. The same is true for cabinet officials. Tom Daschle, President Obama's first choice as Health and Human Services Secretary, withdrew his nomination following the concerns raised about possible ethical violations and tax evasions, ironically stemming from his service in the Senate.

The Supreme Court is shaped by presidential nomination and Senate approval. It is an important part of the constitutional framework that requires the institutions of the federal government to come together in the common cause of framing, passing and adjudicating the laws which structure the framework of American public life. In establishing their independence from one another at the same time as making them interact with each other, a constantly changing political dynamic is created. Nowhere is this better seen than by tracing the shifting boundaries of presidential power.

The problem of presidential power

Only one President has ever entered office with both eyes fixed on the future rather than glancing occasionally over one shoulder at the past. George Washington had only to live up to his own reputation, rather than be judged against a standard of political leadership that many of his successors have aspired to reach but which only a handful have been deemed to achieve. Indeed, the fact that few Presidents are counted in his company is in some respects George Washington's fault. On taking office in April 1789, his task was to map out the parameters of his powers. These had been only briefly outlined in the Constitution, partly because it had been anticipated that Washington could be trusted to take on this challenge. The new President observed correctly that "I walk on untrodden ground."

After specifying the process by which the President is elected, the Constitution therefore defines merely one role, only one responsibility and just three formal powers, before outlining the circumstances under which the Executive can be removed from office. The role is as Commander-in-Chief of the nation's armed forces; the responsibility is to report to the Legislature annually on the state of the union; and the powers are of pardon, of appointment to offices in the federal government and, in certain circumstances, to convene or adjourn Congress. It is not an exhaustive job description.

Many of Washington's actions created a precedent. His acceptance speech on being sworn into office established the tradition of the inaugural address that launches a new administration. His decision to serve for two terms was respected by his successors (not all of whom achieved that ambition) until Franklin Roosevelt ignored it. Subsequently Washington's view that it was enough to serve eight years in the presidency prevailed in a constitutional amendment passed some 154 years after he left office. He established the Departments of State, the Treasury and War (in 1947 renamed as the Department of Defense, but no less belligerent) as well as the Attorney General's Office. These remain the key appointments in a President's Cabinet. Washington's "Farewell Address," nowadays still read annually into the Senate record, endures as an influence in shaping American views of the nation's rightful place in international relations. He is rightly regarded as a political colossus among his peers.

Washington, however, is unique. Famous for being first, significant for the precedents and traditions he established and created, his view of presidential power was nevertheless very much of its time: the Executive should provide leadership but try to remain "above politics." Yet even he could not escape the fact that his position was political. As party divisions emerged in the new republic, the President had to take sides. When forced to make his mind up as to whether or not to veto the establishment of a National Bank, Washington invited the opinions of Alexander Hamilton, his Secretary of the Treasury, and Thomas Jefferson, his Secretary of State. Political enemies, Hamilton supported the bank, Jefferson did not. In eventually agreeing with Hamilton, the President became a partisan. It was not a role that Washington relished: it was with reluctance that he agreed to run for re-election and with relief that he relinquished the office at the end of his second term.

Moreover, the office that he gave up was not exactly large. Washington employed more workers at his private estate at Mount Vernon than he had to help carry out his official duties as President of the United States. Rightly celebrated for guiding the infant federal republic through its critical early years, Washington's presidency affords an initial glimpse into the problem of presidential power. Constitutionally limited, it has subsequently expanded as America has demanded that its Chief Executive takes on an increasingly political as well as symbolic role as leader of the nation.

Among Washington's peers, it was his immediate successor, John Adams, who confronted an increasingly partisan and hostile Congress without the reservoir of goodwill and prestige that had attached to his illustrious predecessor. Adams created another precedent: the first President to run for a second term and lose. It was left to Thomas Jefferson, the nation's third Chief Executive, to explore the contemporary limits of presidential power, ignoring constitutional niceties in seizing the opportunity to add to America's territory. The Louisiana Purchase in 1803 was not simply a shrewd piece of bargaining that enabled the United States to acquire from France the land that would fuel its westward expansion. In acting decisively without consulting Congress, Jefferson demonstrated the presidency could take the political initiative and provide leadership at a critical moment in the nation's development. Congress subsequently ratified his action, but equally important was the fact that Jefferson, the apostle of limited government, had felt able to act at all.

LOUISIANA PURCHASE

The Louisiana Purchase dramatically increased the territory of the United States. The land bought from France for $15 million secured American trade through the port of New Orleans and far more besides. Although President Jefferson by his own admission acted beyond the limits of the powers granted to the President by the Constitution, he did so both in the interests of national security and to open up the potential for expansion to the west. Congress and the American people endorsed his action after it was announced, symbolically, on July 4, 1803.

Among those who occupied the White House after Jefferson and before Franklin Roosevelt, there were relatively few who, either through force of personality or necessity of circumstance, proved able to impose themselves on the office. Andrew Jackson exploited the fact that the Executive is the sole federal office that can claim to represent a national constituency and also a national mandate. He was able to dominate Washington politics to an unprecedented degree, winning important constitutional battles over the nullification crisis which threatened the survival of the union, and over the establishment of a national bank, which he implacably opposed. Historians of the period were right to call it "the Age of Jackson."

Abraham Lincoln expanded presidential power in reaction to the secession crisis and a Civil War that threatened to sweep away the national government altogether. In the twentieth century, Theodore Roosevelt and Woodrow Wilson set the tone for presidential activism in domestic and foreign policy alike. Together they presided over the so-called "progressive era" when the federal government became more actively involved in promoting social and economic reforms to moderate the excesses of unregulated capitalist enterprise. It was Roosevelt who began to flex America's increasing power on the world stage and it was Wilson who led the country into the First World War.

First elected in 1932, Franklin Roosevelt presided over the creation of the so-called "modern presidency" in response to the political challenges he faced as the United States confronted a series of national and international crises that started with the Wall Street Crash in 1929 and continued with the outbreak of the Second World War a decade later. Since FDR's time as Chief Executive, moreover, it has been the President's actions as Commander-in-Chief in times of war that has focused attention on the expansion of presidential power. As America's intervention in the Vietnam War drew to its divisive and controversial close, seeking a scapegoat, the historian Arthur Schlesinger Jr. coined the term "Imperial Presidency" to describe an Executive that had slipped the chains of the Constitution to act in a manner that checks and balances had proven insufficient to control.

The Constitution requires the President to ask Congress for a Declaration of War. Yet since Franklin Roosevelt's request for it to do so following what he called the "day that will live in infamy" that marked the Japanese attack on Pearl Harbor, no President has asked the Legislature to decide formally whether to commit the nation to military action overseas. Instead, in Korea, Vietnam, the Persian Gulf, Afghanistan and Iraq – to name the most prominent examples of America's involvement in international conflicts since the Second World War – Congress has provided supportive resolutions rather than fulfilling its constitutional role of debating and deciding on the merits of a presidential request to commit the nation to war.

Schlesinger argued that after a world war that had seen the Executive "resurgent" in accumulating the powers essential to achieve victory against Germany and Japan, followed by the conflict in Korea in which it had been "ascendant," it was during America's involvement in Vietnam that the presidency had become "rampant." Lyndon Johnson and Richard Nixon claimed to act in the interests of national security, pursuing actions that were ultimately catastrophic not only for themselves but also for the nation. Johnson's presidency was destroyed by Vietnam and Nixon's political career ended in the ignominy of resignation to avoid impeachment. The "Imperial Presidency" crashed and burned in the flames of an unwinnable war in Southeast Asia and the all-consuming domestic scandal of Watergate.

Those who had initially exploited the potential inherent in the constitutional role of the President as Commander-in-Chief were Democrats. Franklin Roosevelt set the stage for this expansion of executive power that his last Vice-President and successor, Harry Truman, exercised in Korea in the early years of the Cold War. And it was Lyndon Johnson whose actions in Vietnam provoked Schlesinger's critique. Since Richard Nixon quit the presidency, however, it has been the Republicans who have tried to re-invigorate presidential power. Gerald Ford, Nixon's unelected successor, reacted against congressional attempts to increase its oversight of the Executive's actions following the Watergate scandal and left office warning that the Presidency was "imperiled" because of them. During Ronald Reagan's years in office, the Iran-Contra scandal – an effective privatization of American foreign policy that enabled the White House to fund a proxy war in Nicaragua through trading arms for hostages – demonstrated the extent to which the Executive sought to avoid the increased scrutiny of a Congress reluctant to support military intervention overseas. In his inaugural address, George H.W. Bush called for an end to the political divisiveness that had marked the relations between the White House and Capitol Hill, but that hostility only increased during Bill Clinton's time in office, fueled by partisans from Bush's own party who resented his defeat in the 1992 election. After the Republicans recaptured the White House in 2000, elements of the new administration were ideologically committed to the re-assertion of presidential power. Over the subsequent eight years, they renewed the fears of their political opponents that George W. Bush was a President who once again over-stepped the boundaries of constitutional restraint.

For many Republicans the primacy of presidential power rests on their conviction that the Constitution allows the development of the "Unitary Executive": a presidency that in effect should have control of all the activities undertaken by the federal government. Dick Cheney was among those who advocated this perspective aggressively to promote the unchecked use of presidential power. He had been Gerald Ford's White House chief of staff in the immediate aftermath of Watergate and, after serving as George H.W. Bush's defense secretary, he re-emerged in 2000 as the Republican Vice-President – a position in which he exercised unprecedented influence. After the terrorist attacks of September 11, 2001, he became a driving force behind the assertion of executive power. The stage was set for another performance of the drama of the "Imperial Presidency" with a familiar final act: George W. Bush left office with an approval rating hovering around twenty-eight percent, far lower in public esteem than LBJ (forty-nine percent) and almost as vilified as Richard Nixon (twenty-four percent).

George W. Bush's decisions in the aftermath of 9/11 – to declare a global "war on terror," to invade Afghanistan and topple the Taliban regime and to fight a war in Iraq, the outcome of which slid rapidly beyond his control – shaped the subsequent course of his administration. It is unsuccessful military action that fatally corrodes the nation's faith in a President's capacity to lead. The contemporary problem of presidential power may thus be reduced to a straightforward observation. Presidential authority rests on political credibility. Once lost, it is difficult to regain. Moreover, taking the nation to war is a high stakes political gamble.

When the nation faces a crisis it looks to its President to provide leadership. In such circumstances, Congress may defer to the Executive, as it did to Abraham Lincoln during the Civil War and to Franklin Roosevelt during the economic depression of the 1930s and then after the Japanese attack on Pearl Harbor had brought America into the Second World War. At the same time, however, if the President is judged to have flouted his constitutional authority, Congress reacts against the institution as much as against its occupant. In this way, Barack Obama entered the Oval Office as the successor to a President whose conduct in office had provoked an outcry from his critics, wary that once more the Executive had assumed too much power. With the nation embroiled in unpopular wars, Obama could not expect the same degree of deference that had been allowed Lincoln as Commander-in-Chief, nor, with the global economic crisis unraveling, did he have the same dominant authority over Congress as had been enjoyed by Franklin Roosevelt. If his inheritance was the most toxic of modern times, his task was also the most complex: exercising presidential power within its constitutional limitations when the times called for decisive leadership.

Judicial power and judicial politics

The American Constitution details the powers of Congress, outlines the responsibilities of the President, but is undeniably vague when it comes to the role that the Supreme Court should play in the federal government. It merely announces that "the judicial power of the United States shall be vested in one Supreme Court and in such inferior courts as the Congress may from time to time ordain and establish." It took time, therefore, for the Court to realize its potential in exercising its judicial power in ways that have profoundly impacted upon the nation's politics and which continue to shape American society.

In 1789, the Senate's first ever item of legislative business was to consider the Judiciary Act. The United States was divided into thirteen judicial districts organized into three "circuits." The six members of the Supreme Court, one of whom became Chief Justice, were obliged not only to hold sessions in the nation's capital but also to "ride circuit," meeting twice each year in each judicial district. This practice continued for just over a hundred years. The peripatetic life required of the Justices, particularly during the period when traveling around the country was far from easy, was sometimes a disincentive to joining the Court.

Moreover, in the early years of the federal government, the Supreme Court did not have much to do. John Jay, the first Chief Justice, who served from 1789 to 1795, took time out in 1792 to campaign unsuccessfully to become Governor of New York. Two years later he was sent by George Washington to Britain to negotiate the treaty that bears his name, resolving some of the issues that had soured relations between the two countries following the end of the War of Independence. Many argued indeed that Jay's Treaty averted another war between the two nations. In his absence abroad, his political aspirations finally were fulfilled when he was elected as New York's Governor and he was able to resign his judicial appointment.

When Jay left the Supreme Court, Congress was not in session and so an interim successor was appointed. In an early example of the recurrent phenomenon that Justices, once appointed, may behave in ways that Presidents might not predict when they nominate them, Washington's choice to become the second Chief Justice, John Rutledge, made a controversial speech denouncing his predecessor's treaty negotiations. Amid allegations of mental instability and alcohol abuse, he was not confirmed when the Senate eventually considered his appointment. He resigned after six months. Oliver Ellsworth, who succeeded Rutledge, emulated Jay in leading a delegation across the Atlantic in 1799, this time to France to undertake diplomatic negotiations with Napoleon. His health suffered as a result and in 1801 he too resigned.

Ellsworth quit the Court at a critical time. The President, John Adams, had been defeated in his bid for re-election and Thomas Jefferson, who had won the controversial election of 1800 and who was then branded by the defeated Federalist party as a dangerous radical, was about to enter the White House. Adams, however, could still nominate the new Chief Justice of the Supreme Court before he left office. He turned to his Secretary of State, John Marshall, whose appointment was ratified by the Senate on February 4, 1801, a month before Jefferson's inauguration. So it was that Marshall, a distant cousin but a lifelong political opponent of the new President, administered the oath of office to Jefferson and began the process of molding the Court into a powerful counterweight to the other institutions of the federal government.

A landmark decision in the history of the Court is the one which was handed down in 1803 in the case of *Marbury v. Madison*. In one of his first opinions as Chief Justice, Marshall asserted the power of the Court to decide the constitutionality of the nation's laws. Ironically it was his own lack of time-management skills while Secretary of State that precipitated the events leading to Marshall's most significant judicial decision. After the election of 1800 and as the presidency of John Adams entered its final days, the Federalist party, having lost its grip on the White House, attempted to tighten its control over the Judiciary by appointing a number of judges to the federal bench. The process to create these so-called "midnight judges" was carried out hastily and haphazardly. In the Department of State, it was ultimately Marshall, continuing in this role while assuming his new position as Chief Justice, who was responsible for the necessary paperwork. As time ran out for the Federalists, one of their nominees, William Marbury, failed to receive the documents necessary for him to become a judge before the new Republican administration took office. As President, Jefferson withheld Marbury's commission, arguing that he was not bound to honor the previous administration's judicial appointments if they had not been properly executed in time. The new Secretary of State, James Madison, refused to deliver Marbury's official papers, without which he could not take up his position as Justice of the Peace in the District of Columbia.

The Supreme Court was called upon to decide who was in the right and who was in the wrong. Marshall was confronted with a tricky political problem. If he agreed with Marbury that Madison was legally bound to deliver the papers, he risked an early and potentially explosive confrontation with the new President. On the other hand, to agree with the administration's actions would diminish the status of the Court within the constitutional system. Marshall's decision neatly finessed his dilemma. He argued that Marbury had a right to his commission but that the Supreme Court could not force Madison to deliver the necessary papers because if it did so it would itself be acting unconstitutionally.

This neat solution rested on Marshall's interpretation of what the Court could and could not do. Marbury had taken his case against Madison directly to the Supreme Court. Marshall argued that was a mistake. The Constitution envisaged that the Supreme Court would not have original jurisdiction – deciding cases for the first time – except in a limited number of circumstances. Marbury had directly petitioned the Court to force Madison to carry out his responsibility, assuming that the Judiciary Act of 1789 had given it that power. That allowed Marshall to see a way out of his political problem. He argued an important legal and constitutional point. There was a conflict between what the Constitution allowed of the Court, and what the Judiciary Act required it to do.

The Supreme Court was primarily a court of appeal. So it should not assume the power of original jurisdiction in Marbury's case in order to issue a writ against Madison. Although Marshall supported Marbury's claim in principle, in practice, by declaring that the relevant section of the Judiciary Act under which his case was brought was in fact unconstitutional, he effectively avoided forcing Madison's hand. More significant still was the legal precedent set by this decision. Marshall asserted that the Supreme Court should have the final say on the constitutionality of laws.

The decision in *Marbury v. Madison* therefore established two important principles that continue to define the authority and the role of the Supreme Court within the American political system: judicial review and the supremacy of the Constitution. Marshall annexed the power of judicial review to the Court simply by claiming that "It is emphatically the province and duty of the Judicial Department to say what the law is." Moreover, "if two laws conflict with each other, the Courts must decide on the operation of each." In Marshall's opinion, "the Constitution is superior to any ordinary act of the Legislature" and so "the Constitution, and not such ordinary act, must govern the case to which they both apply." The Chief Justice was able to define a role for the Court that cemented its status within the hierarchy of checks and balances necessary to the operation of the separation of powers. Now the Court would decide cases on the basis of its interpretation of the Constitution and would, if necessary, declare the actions of the Legislature and the Executive unconstitutional.

It was a power that to be effective was best used sparingly. In the sixty years after Marshall's landmark decision, the Court used it on only one further occasion. In 1857, in the case of *Dred Scott v. Sanford*, Marshall's successor, the southerner, Roger Taney, who had been appointed by Andrew Jackson, delivered the Court's opinion that the 1820 Missouri Compromise was unconstitutional. Intense political negotiations had gone on in Congress to draw the line as to where slavery might be extended in the western territories acquired through the Louisiana Purchase. Now, and thirty-seven years after the event, the Supreme Court decided that Congress could not assume the constitutional power to leg-islate in order to prevent the spread of slavery. The decision inflamed the sectional tensions within the United States that eventually led to the outbreak of the Civil War.

The ramifications of the Dred Scott decision confirm, if such confirmation is needed, that the Supreme Court's rulings can have important political consequences. That has been the case in particular when it tackles fundamental issues that impact on the liberty of the individual within American society. Consider civil rights. The Court's decision in *Plessy v. Ferguson* (1896) legit-imized the practices of racial apartheid in the American South that persisted, under the euphemism of "separate but equal," until it overturned its own ruling in *Brown v. Board of Education* (1954).

In *Roe v. Wade* (1973), which found in favor of a woman's right to abortion, the Court sparked the "right to life" versus "right to choose" debate that has been an often bitter and some-times violent fault-line in American political discourse ever since that decision. During the 1980s, when President Reagan, a firm supporter of the "right to life," appointed judges to the Supreme Court, he faced criticism that a "litmus test" for his nominees was their attitude on the issue of abortion. In 1983, while still President, Reagan took the time to send an article to the *Human Life Review* in which he argued that:

> as an act of 'raw judicial power' … the decision by the seven-man majority in *Roe* v. *Wade* has so far been made to stick. But the Court's decision has by no means settled the debate. Instead, *Roe* v. *Wade* has become a continuing prod to the con-science of the nation.

A few months after Reagan had left office in 1989, the Supreme Court delivered its decision in the case of *Webster v. Reproductive Health Services*. Sandra Day O'Connor, whom Reagan had appointed to the Court, was initially among the five justices who were in favor of a decision that would have overturned *Roe v. Wade*, but then changed her mind. The Court re-affirmed its *Roe* decision by a five to four vote. In 1992, in its decision in *Casey v. Planned Parenthood* the Supreme Court once again endorsed its *Roe* opinion that abortion laws were constitutional. O'Connor joined two other conservatives on the Court, David Souter and Anthony Kennedy, in arguing that to overturn the 1973 decision would cause "damage to the Court's legitimacy and to the rule of law." Yet this is a controversy that refuses to go away and one in which the Supreme Court has been and will be continually involved.

More recently, in 2008, in the case of *Boumediene v. Bush*, the Court ruled that the Bush administration should not deny those detained at Guantanamo Bay in Cuba having their cases heard in federal courts. Prisoners had constitutionally protected habeas corpus rights. A year later, however, as the Obama administration was becoming embroiled in controversy over how it might close the camp in Cuba, the Court refused to review a lower court's dismissal of *Rasul v. Rumsfeld*, a case brought by several former detainees who alleged they had been tortured while in Guantanamo. On March 1, 2010, moreover, the Court announced that it would not hear a case scheduled for later that month concerning Chinese Muslims who had been imprisoned for eight years in Guantanamo. *Kiyemba v. Obama* raised the difficult issue of whether a detainee freed through exercising the right of habeas corpus could be released into the United States. Instead of debating that issue, the Court sent the case back to the lower courts. Such decisions show that what the Supreme Court will not consider may be as politically charged as its choice of the cases that it can use to try to mesh the constitutional framework and the prevailing sentiments of American society.

Individual Supreme Court justices have often proven to be thorns in the side of Presidents – sometimes even of those who appointed them. In 1902, Theodore Roosevelt nominated Oliver Wendell Holmes Jr. to the Court. Holmes, who served with distinction for thirty years, nevertheless defied the President in his opinion on an anti-trust case, prompting Roosevelt to let it be known that "I could carve out of a banana a judge with more backbone than that." In the 1930s, his cousin Franklin would find the federal Judiciary increasingly stubborn in opposing his New Deal legislation. However, his proposal to "pack the Court" with his supporters represented such a transparent attempt to short-circuit the Constitutional separation of powers that Congress refused to countenance it.

Who governs?

In 1878, the British Liberal politician William Gladstone, who with his conservative counterpart Benjamin Disraeli dominated the nation's political life during the late nineteenth century, described the American Constitution as "the most wonderful work ever struck off by the brain and purpose of man. It has had a century of trial … and … has certainly proved the sagacity of the constructors and the stubborn strength of the fabric." Yet would he have wanted to have been President of the United States of America rather than Prime Minister of Britain? For Gladstone also confessed himself puzzled as to "why the American people should permit their entire existence to be continually disturbed by the business of the presidential elections." During his lifetime only six Presidents won re-election. James Madison was President when Gladstone was born in December 1809. On his death in May 1898, William McKinley was in the White House and Gladstone had lived through the administrations of twenty-one different Presidents. Contrast the Liberal leader's own political career. He was first elected to the House of Commons in 1832, the same year that Andrew Jackson became President. He made his last speech there in March 1894 when Grover Cleveland was about to enter the second year of his second term in office. Moreover, for almost fourteen of his sixty-two years in Parliament, Gladstone was Prime Minister. In terms of his legislative longevity as well as the time he spent holding the highest executive office in the country, his experience, admittedly unique in British terms, is nevertheless unparalleled when compared with contemporaries across the Atlantic.

Time horizons are important. Since the twenty-second amendment was passed in the aftermath of Franklin Roosevelt's precedent-breaking twelve years in office, on first entering the White House, Presidents know they have, barring unforeseen tragedy, four years there. That may be followed by a fight for re-election. However long they are in the presidency, they must seek to impose their authority in a constitutional system expressly designed to frustrate the use of power in order to prevent its abuse. That impacts on their political careers. Among Franklin Roosevelt's successors, from Harry Truman to George W. Bush, five out of eleven Presidents have been re-elected but only four have successfully completed two terms in office. If the contemporary President's tenure in office is unpredictable beyond four years and impermissible beyond eight, so too are the outcomes when he presents his legislative agenda to Congress. Rarely has a President been able to cajole Congress – even one in which his party is in control of both the House of Representatives and the Senate – into unqualified support for his campaign commitments. It takes special circumstances (Roosevelt during the Depression) or a particular skill (Lyndon Johnson's persuasive ability) for the President to consistently dominate the legislative process.

It follows that the key political relationship for any President is the one he forges with Congress. In this respect Barack Obama, the first President since John F. Kennedy to move directly from the Senate to the White House, demonstrated considerable political skill and sensitivity during his first months in office. The circumstances of his election and the political coalition that he mobilized behind his agenda for "change we can believe in" seemed to symbolize the end of the so-called "Reagan Revolution." In 1980 the election of the former Hollywood actor to the White House ushered in an era of limited government and tax-cuts, finding favor with those former Democrats who had changed allegiance to the Republicans. Ironically, however, Obama's and Reagan's approaches to Congress proved remarkably similar. Rather than present the House of Representatives and the Senate with detailed legislation for them to approve, like his Republican predecessor, Obama set the broad parameters of policy and invited Congress to fill in the details. His initial overtures toward bi-partisanship in the face of the economic crisis that he had inherited on entering office proved unsuccessful. Nevertheless, the Obama administration was able to put together a congressional coalition that supported a "stimulus package" for the economy that the President was happy to adopt as his own and which he signed into law within a month of taking office. A similar strategy enabled Obama to claim success in achieving healthcare reform, finally approved by Congress in March 2010.

Perspectives are inevitably influenced by knowledge of the recent past and the remorseless electoral timetable. The President enters office with the concern that even if his party has a majority in the Legislature on the day of his inauguration, less than two years later, the November mid-term elections can change the political landscape dramatically. Ronald Reagan in 1982, Bill Clinton in 1994 and Barack Obama in 2010 saw their party majorities in one or both houses of Congress evaporate during their first term in office, and in 2006 George W. Bush experienced a similar reversal of political fortunes during his second administration.

With the entire House of Representatives elected every two years, time horizons there remain naturally short.

Although incumbency brings advantages, individual members know that if they lose support within their districts, there are limited opportunities to regain it. Collectively, however, since 1900 both Republicans and Democrats have managed to retain control of the House for extended periods of time. Republican majorities held sway there for twenty-four of the first thirty years of the century. Thereafter came a period of Democrat dominance which lasted, apart from two brief interruptions, for sixty years. It was followed by the twelve years of Republican majorities in the House that occurred between the mid-term elections of 1992 and 2006. That history was shaped in no small measure by the electoral earthquake which took place in 1932 at a time of economic collapse and the onset of the Great Depression. Following their mauling at the polls, it took the Republicans fourteen years before they once again were able to command a majority in the House. Having won just 117 seats in the year that Franklin Roosevelt first captured the White House and in 1936, having been reduced to eighty-eight members in the House, it took time to rebuild the party's electoral fortunes in the Legislature. The Republican mid-term victory in 1946, when the party gained fifty-five seats in the House of Representatives and twelve in the Senate, made them the majority party in Congress. Yet President Truman turned this political defeat to his advantage. Two years later he won an upset victory in his bid for re-election in a contest which Thomas Dewey, his Republican opponent, was widely expected to win. Truman accused the "do-nothing 80th Congress" of preventing him from enacting his legislative program. The electorate backed the incumbent of the White House in his battle with Capitol Hill. The Democrats took back control of Congress.

After sixteen of the twenty-five congressional elections held between 1950 and the end of the century, the President woke up to a House of Representatives controlled by the opposition party. In recent times, therefore, the dynamics of the relationship between the President and the House have been shaped by that prospect. Between the end of the Second World War and Obama's election in 2008, only three Presidents – John F. Kennedy, Lyndon Johnson and Jimmy Carter; Democrats all – have had their party in the majority in the House of Representatives for the entire duration of their administrations. Kennedy's presidency was tragically curtailed and Carter's four years in the White House were marked by his failure to gain the support of Democrats in Congress. Only Lyndon Johnson, whose political skills had been honed by his time as majority leader in the Senate and who knew how to win support in Congress, was able to take full legislative advantage of this comparatively rare political occurrence in pursuing his ambition to create his "Great Society."

Time horizons in the Senate are longer, as, once elected, Senators have six years in office. While one party's ability to control both the Executive and the Legislature simultaneously has proven increasingly difficult to sustain, within Congress, since 1900, divided government has been rare. Following the mid-term elections of 1910 and 1930 and then only for the life-time of a single Congress, the Republicans retained their majority in the Senate while losing it in the House. The two Houses of Congress were controlled by different parties after the 1980 elections when the Republicans, riding the coat-tails of Ronald Reagan, captured the Senate and remained in the majority there until the mid-term elections of 1986. In the 2010 mid-terms, the Democrats lost the House but retained control of the Senate.

Party majorities in the Senate are brittle, particularly in recent times. After the 2000 election, the Republicans and the Democrats had fifty seats each and tied votes were decided by the vote of the Senate's presiding officer, Vice-President Dick Cheney. The Republicans then managed to improve their position after both the 2002 and 2004 elections. Two years later, the Democrats were able to regain almost all their lost ground and with the support of two independents reclaimed control of the Senate. The Republican electoral debacle of 2008 allowed their rivals to consolidate their position, although they still fell just short of achieving the elusive target of a filibuster-proof sixty-seat majority there, the number of votes necessary to block the minority party following the Senate tradition of unlimited debate in order to stop measures ever coming to a vote. The Republicans fought back in the 2010 mid-term elections and gained an additional six Senate seats.

For the Judiciary, time horizons are different. In April 2010 the longest serving member of the Court, John Paul Stevens – appointed to it by President Gerald Ford and having served for over three decades – announced his retirement. At that time, five other of the current Supreme Court justices had been nominated by Republican Presidents and three by Democrats. John Roberts, appointed by George W. Bush to the court at the age of fifty, is the third youngest Chief Justice in American history, after John Jay (forty-four) and John Marshall (forty-five when appointed). Like Marshall, he may seek to influence the Court's direction for many years. Nevertheless, at present a delicate political balance has been maintained. Currently, Roberts allies himself with three fellow conservative judges on the one hand ranged against four liberal-leaning colleagues who now include Sonia Sotomayor and Elena Kagan, both appointed by President Obama. The "swing vote" may remain with Justice Anthony Kennedy, appointed by Ronald Reagan and generally thought of as a conservative, who on occasions may nevertheless agree with the liberals.

Deciding upon the composition of the Court thus involves the President reaching a political accommodation with the Senate in the knowledge that Supreme Court Justices may be the tortoises of the American constitutional system compared to the political hares in the White House. For Senators, the time horizons are different again. In 2005, one of the five members of the Senate Judiciary Committee who refused to support John Roberts' nomination was none other than the late Edward Kennedy who by then could himself look back at a political career not quite as long as Gladstone's, but nevertheless which approached half a century of public service. It proved to be one of Kennedy's last congressional votes. Moreover, six months after he died, in January 2010, the Democrat party lost control of his Senate seat in Massachusetts. It was a sober political reminder that within the system of "separated institutions sharing powers," when an election takes place, it is public opinion that matters most of all.

3

Political parties and the perpetual campaign

Two political parties, the Democrats and the Republicans, dominate modern American politics. The Democrats have the deepest roots in the nation's history, stretching back to the 1830s and Andrew Jackson's time, whereas the Republicans began to organize in the 1850s, in the decade before the Civil War. However the names of both can be traced back to the founding period. American parties have one over-riding concern: to win elections. Their ideological outlooks have therefore proved adaptable to the changing priorities of the voters whose support they must gain. During the last 150 years, the Democrats have moved from being the party that viewed federal power with suspicion, particularly in their defense of the southern states' right to maintain slavery, to the party which supported government intervention to promote greater equality and social justice. The Republicans began as a party that opposed the extension of slavery, became the party of big business, and nowadays is the home for those of moderate conservative and more extreme fundamentalist religious views. American parties are broad coalitions, constantly re-inventing themselves in the pursuit of electoral success.

Once the Constitution had been ratified and the first federal elections had been held it kick-started two further developments in American politics: elections for public office and the formation of the political parties, which after a stuttering start came to dominate the democratic process. Both these developments were significant in defining the contours of American politics. Moreover, the existence of the Electoral College influences candidates and their parties in shaping strategies and determining outcomes in a political system in which the presidency has become the biggest prize.

America's only national election takes place every four years, but campaigning never ends. Aspiring presidential candidates embark on a political journey that begins as the dust settles on the previous contest. First they have to capture their party's nomination. That takes them to the battlegrounds of the caucuses and the primaries. After the Iowa caucuses comes the New Hampshire primary, then "Super Tuesday" when a number of states hold primary elections on the same day. The calendar of caucuses and primaries continues. For the successful presidential hopeful who manages to gain enough support within the party to win its presidential nomination, it is on to the national party convention. This meeting of the party faithful, which takes place at the end of the nominating process, rallies support behind the successful candidate. The focus of the election pivots from the fight that has gone on between rivals within the same party during the primary season toward the looming battle with the rival party's nominee. This intense final stage of the campaign culminates in November with the presidential election itself.

CAUCUSES AND PRIMARIES

Caucuses and primary elections are part of the nominating process by which parties select candidates for office. A caucus is a small gathering of party members where discussions take place to agree on which candidate should be supported at the nominating convention. A primary is an election that takes place to achieve a similar objective but which involves balloting on a statewide basis.

Communication is key. The role of the media can be critical in the shaping of public opinion. Those who run for national office nowadays must accept that the line between their public and private lives is practically erased as the campaign unfolds. The media spotlight may turn on a candidate with disastrous results: Senator Gary Hart's 1998 campaign imploded because of newspaper allegations that he was having an extra-marital affair. In the aftermath of the Watergate scandal, public skepticism was heightened by Hart's vehement denials of infidelity. A century earlier, Grover Cleveland had responded to campaign rumors that he was the father of an illegitimate son by telling the truth and accepting paternity. He went on to win the presidency. Hart eventually admitted his affair, observing that he "wasn't running for sainthood." He lost the New Hampshire primary to Michael Dukakis and his campaign collapsed.

The established formulas of political communication through public appearances, "stump speeches," media advertisements and debates help to galvanize support. However, technological innovation, particularly if it allows unmediated access to potential voters, can also deliver a decisive advantage in enabling candidates to control the information accessed by their potential supporters. In 2008, Barack Obama's campaign exploited new means of communication and in particular the use of social networking sites to help galvanize a grass roots movement that could be built into a formidable political machine. If the conventions of "Facebook" required Obama to reveal his tastes in music, film and literature, they also allowed him to fashion a populist image that resonated with his "virtual" friends, many of whom became active in his campaign.

In battling for the nomination, candidates must first capture the imagination of their parties before going on to fight the election. Moreover, once in the White House, unlike a British Prime Minister, the President does not confront a "leader of the opposition" throughout his time in office. If a party's nominee as presidential candidate is regarded as its nominal head, it is a tempo-rary position that may not endure beyond the election campaign. Indeed, since the Second World War only two losing candidates, Adlai Stevenson for the Democrats and Richard Nixon for the Republicans, have been given a second chance at contesting a presidential election. Stevenson failed, but Nixon, having been defeated in 1960, won the White House eight years later.

Presidential campaigns do not only expose the strengths and weaknesses of candidates as they try to sell themselves in the "retail politics" of the campaign trail. They also demonstrate the critical role of political parties in structuring how America's democratic process works. Since the Civil War, no third party has emerged to challenge the Democrat and Republican strangle-hold on elective offices in the United States. This has been most evident every four years in the contest for the White House. On those occasions when there have been challenges to the two party dominance – Theodore Roosevelt's "Bull Moose" party in 1912, George Wallace's American Independent Party in 1968 or Ross Perot's Reform Party in 1992 – it has been to support a maverick candidate. Third party candidates have very little chance of success, other than in splitting the votes for one of their rivals. Roosevelt ran ahead of Robert Taft, siphoning Republican votes away from the incumbent President and presenting the presi-dency to his Democrat rival, Woodrow Wilson. Yet the contem-porary dominance of the Democrat and Republican parties is not a development that would have been either anticipated or welcomed among those who wrote the Constitution. Instead, their predominant view was that parties were a threat to the survival of a democratic republic.

Coming to the party

In his celebrated Farewell Address to the new nation as he left office in 1796, George Washington warned "in the most solemn manner, against the baneful effects of the spirit of party generally." In his mind, the existence of parties was a threat that could subvert the ideals of a republic based upon the idea of representative government. James Madison had designed the Constitution to "break and control the violence of faction." Less than a decade after its ratification, however, the United States, according to its first President, should beware "the alternate domination of one faction over another, sharpened by the spirit of revenge, natural to party dissensions." This, thought Washington, would lead to political instability which could then easily be exploited by potential demagogues. Americans might be tempted "to seek repose in the absolute power of an individual" and the leader of a faction would be able to come to power "on the ruins of public liberty." Such a heartfelt warning, coming from the nation's first Chief Executive, demonstrated the depth of contemporary concerns that political parties subverted the ideals of the revolutionary era.

Washington's opposition to political parties was based upon his experience as President. He had been the reluctant witness to their emergence in the United States. In his first administration, he had appointed Alexander Hamilton as Secretary of the Treasury and Thomas Jefferson as Secretary of State. They had fundamentally different views about the extent of the powers that the Constitution gave to the new federal government and how they should be used. Hamilton, whose political talents proved better than his ability to aim a gun (he would die after dueling with Aaron Burr, then Vice-President of the United States), saw how to organize support in Congress to approve the legislative initiatives that he orchestrated from his position within the executive branch at the Treasury Department. In turn, Jefferson's "great collaborator," James Madison, who had taken a seat in the House of Representatives, started to coordinate opposition to what both Virginians agreed was Hamilton's attempt to centralize power. During his second term Washington had struggled to remain "above politics" in adopting a non-partisan approach to his role as Chief Executive. Instead he became identified increasingly with what became accepted as the Federalist party, as was his loyal Vice-President, John Adams.

Writing from Amsterdam to his Massachusetts friend, Jonathan Jackson, in 1780, Adams had observed that:

> there is nothing which I dread so much as a division of the republic into two great parties, each arranged under its leader, and concerting measures in opposition to each other. This, in my humble apprehension, is to be dreaded as the greatest political evil under our Constitution.

By the time he ran for the Presidency in 1796, however, it was as the Federalist party's candidate. Thomas Jefferson, his former political ally in the Continental Congress during the War of Independence, now opposed him as leader of the Democrat-Republican party (it was confusingly known by either name or sometimes both). Adams won, but with Jefferson as the runner-up in the Electoral College, for the first and only time in American history, the President and the Vice-President belonged to different parties – although to avoid daily confrontations Jefferson retreated rapidly to his Monticello estate and left Adams alone in the White House. When Jefferson returned to the political fray, defeating Adams in the presidential election of 1800, it was the first time that the United States witnessed a peaceful transition of power between two opposing political parties. In itself this was a vital step in entrenching democratic practice. The Federalists accepted their defeat. The new President was magnanimous in victory. In his inaugural address he asserted that "We are all republicans – we are all federalists." Thereafter the first American party system collapsed, with the Federalists all but vanishing from the political scene.

For over two decades, federal politics was characterized by what became known during President Monroe's administration as the "era of good feelings." In 1824, however, good feelings turned bad in a bitterly fought and controversial presidential election. Andrew Jackson, aspiring to be the first President not to come from Virginia or to be called Adams, failed in his first attempt to win the White House. Four years later, he was successful as leader of the new Democrat party, which had been organized expressly to elect him to the presidency. Democrats also dominated the congressional elections of that year. Jackson's success ushered in a new era of party rivalries. Opposition to Jackson organized in the form of the Whig party, which managed to win two presidential elections − in 1840 and 1848 − although on both occasions its successful candidates, William Henry Harrison and Zachary Taylor, died in office. During the 1850s the Whigs disappeared, to be replaced by the Republicans, who, after Abraham Lincoln's election in 1860, subsequently dominated presidential politics, winning twelve out of the sixteen elections held between 1868 and 1932 and occupying the White House for all but sixteen of those sixty-four years.

"ERA OF GOOD FEELINGS"

The "era of good feelings" was the way a Boston newspaper described the political atmosphere in the United States following the inauguration of President Monroe in 1816. His election had destroyed the last vestiges of the Federalist party and the lack of organized opposition to the Democrat-Republicans led to a period of one party dominance which came to an end when factional disputes broke out following the controversial presidential election of 1824.

American political parties have organized primarily for electoral purposes. Their sights are most often fixed upon controlling the Executive: the contests between Jefferson and John Adams and subsequently between his son, John Quincy and Jackson were personal political struggles in which parties brought structure and discipline to the electoral process. Abraham Lincoln established the Republicans as an enduring presence in the political landscape of the United States, notably in the White House. Following the victory of Ulysses S. Grant in the first election after the Civil War, seventeen out of the subsequent twenty-seven Presidents have represented the party of Lincoln.

The longevity of the Republicans and the even longer tradition of the Democrats also suggest that it is electoral success rather than ideological consistency that continues to define American political parties. The Civil War proved to be a watershed. The Democrats could no longer defend states' rights to maintain the indefensible institution of slavery. The Republicans, initially the party formed from growing abolitionist sentiment, had achieved their political objective. Over time, therefore, the dominant outlooks of both parties changed even though their names remained the same. After 1865 they molded their appeal to their sense of the prevailing electoral mood as American industrialization gathered pace. A good illustration of this is the way in which, during the early years of the twentieth century, both main parties took up a similar cause. The Republicans, after becoming increasingly identified with the concerns of corporate business during the post-Civil War "Gilded Age" of rapid industrial growth, recognized the need to curb the excesses of capitalist enterprise under the progressive leadership of Theodore Roosevelt (1901–1908). Similarly, from being the party identified with states' rights and the cause of slavery in the South, the Democrats under Woodrow Wilson (1912–1920) then adopted and advanced Roosevelt's contemporary agenda of progressive reform and federal government intervention to promote the economic and social welfare of the nation.

In 1932, the congressional coalition was forged between southern Democrats, conservative on issues of social reform, and their more liberal northern counterparts, in support of the further government interventionism of Franklin Roosevelt's "New Deal." It lasted for over three decades. When President Lyndon Johnson signed the Civil Rights Act into law in 1964, he predicted that he was "signing away the south for fifty years." He was right. White southern Democrats abandoned the party and the Republicans began to win elections in the former Confederacy. At the same time, the Republican party became the home of those who were critical of the levels of government spending that characterized Johnson's "Great Society" programs of social and welfare reform. As Ronald Reagan, a supporter of Franklin Roosevelt in the 1930s, said, "I didn't leave the Democrat Party, it left me." Increasingly opposed to "big government," during the 1980s the Republicans became the advocates for low taxation and less government.

A decade later, the popularity of the "Reagan Revolution" led "New Democrats" under Bill Clinton to advocate for a "third way," which, in the political language of the time, "triangulated" between the public philosophies symbolized by Reagan and Roosevelt that between them had defined domestic politics in the United States for most of the twentieth century. The landslide victory of Barack Obama in 2008, with the Democrats also controlling both the House of Representatives and the Senate, may have suggested that the "Reagan Revolution" had lost its appeal. The American electorate voted for a candidate who promised more active government intervention to tackle the economic recession and problems ranging from the lack of adequate healthcare provision to the environmental issues causing climate change. On the other hand, Obama was unable to build a bi-partisan consensus in Congress to support his ambitious political agenda. In the first year of his presidency opposition to his legislative proposals organized across America from the Tea Party movement, which quickly became an influential and radical force within the Republican party. In the 2010 mid-term elections the President's party took what he called a "shellacking" as voters turned away from the Democrats. Deep fissures continue to lie beneath the surface of America's contemporary political terrain.

TEA PARTY MOVEMENT

Taking inspiration and its name from the 1773 Boston Tea Party, when rebellious colonists raided British ships in Boston harbor and dumped their cargoes of tea overboard in an anti-tax protest, the Tea Party movement achieved national prominence soon after Obama was elected to the White House. It represented a conservative and libertarian backlash against what its supporters saw as Democrat party plans to increase federal government intervention in their daily lives.

Running for the White House: caucuses and primaries

Like the mid-term elections of 2010, the election of Barack Obama in 2008 was an example of a recurring phenomenon in American electoral politics: a major party seeking to capitalize on the prevailing mood of a disgruntled electorate. Yet it was also an extremely risky undertaking. Tracing Obama's path to the presidency is an excellent illustration of how a contemporary bid for the White House can start by defying the political odds and end with an aura of inevitability. His campaign began as an insurgency. The Democrats' nomination had initially seemed to be in the firm grip of Hillary Clinton, whose name recognition and polling support as the primary season approached eclipsed all her potential rivals, the first term Senator from Illinois included. To understand Obama's success it is necessary to appreciate how the change he promised America suffused the way he campaigned. Together with his chief strategist, David Axelrod, and campaign manager, David Plouffe, Obama saw how he could win the nomination through out-maneuvering and out-organizing his opponents in fresh and innovative ways. Winning a party's presidential nomination requires a great deal of thought combined with an obsessive attention to detail. The parties decide the rules of the game, which have become more complex over time. A small but decisive advantage goes to those who take time to master them.

Campaigns for a party's presidential nomination are a marathon steeplechase. Candidates may fall early. The American media delights in betting on candidates as they emerge from the electoral starting blocks, so early successes are seen as crucial in gaining the necessary momentum for a front-runner to leave political rivals behind. It follows that those states which are first to decide their delegates for the national convention receive a disproportionate amount of a candidate's time and a corresponding degree of media attention. From 1920 to the present day, New Hampshire has started the presidential primary season, with the date creeping ever closer to the start of election year. In 2008 it was held on January 8. Since the 1970s, however, an even earlier hurdle in the nominating process has been in place. The Iowa caucuses have now become a crucial early test of a candidate's popularity. The state is the place where aspiring Presidents have their first prolonged exposure to the electorate, the "retail politics" of meeting potential supporters face-to-face in the months leading to the caucus. Winning the Iowa caucuses is regarded as an important symbolic victory: a possible portent of future success.

In 2008, Obama, the former Chicago community organizer, used his talent to the full in achieving an unlikely victory in Iowa. Although he subsequently lost the first primary in New Hampshire, his unanticipated caucus victory – he had emerged as the front-runner only very late in a close-fought campaign – established him as a viable candidate. Moreover, it demonstrated the extent to which his campaign took the caucus system seriously as a source of potential pledged delegates. By the end of the primary season, Hillary Clinton had managed to win in only one of the states that held caucuses. Obama was successful in the other thirteen, thereby gaining a total of 310 pledged delegates at the nominating convention. His eventual margin of victory over Hillary Clinton was 305 delegate votes.

Despite Obama demonstrating the potential of caucuses as a source of delegate support, winning primary elections is still regarded as the key to mounting a successful presidential campaign. It was not always the case. Up to Andrew Jackson's time, it had been the party in Congress who decided who would be candidates for election. After 1828, this power moved to the party's national conventions where, in a less health-conscious age, influential party members gathered in "smoke-filled rooms," emerging to reveal their preferred choice to the delegates whose votes they controlled. In the early twentieth century, however, progressive reforms led to the smoke clearing. A slightly more transparent process was adopted. In 1910 Oregon was the first state to pass legislation requiring a presidential primary election to be held, after which delegates to the national convention were pledged to support a specific candidate. Some states hold "open primaries" in which anyone can vote; in others participation is restricted to registered party members.

The primary system grew fairly rapidly in popularity if rather slowly in influence. It was seen initially as a method of gauging a candidate's potential rather than determining the outcome of the nominating process. In 1952, Dwight Eisenhower took a major step toward becoming the Republican candidate when in the New Hampshire primary he proved more popular than "Mr. Republican," Robert Taft, who many had seen as the party's front-runner. In the same year and in the same state, the incumbent President Truman's defeat by Senator Estes Kefauver from Tennessee was a determining factor persuading him not to run for another term in the White House. In 1960, John F. Kennedy's strong showing in the Democrat primaries, notably in the heavily Protestant state of West Virginia, helped him overcome reservations within the party that a Catholic candidate could not win the presidency.

After 1968, when its rancorous and bitterly divided convention had nominated Lyndon Johnson's Vice-President, Hubert Humphrey, despite widespread support for the anti-Vietnam war candidate Eugene McCarthy, the Democrats set about the reforms which have, since that time, shaped the way the nominating process works. The McGovern-Fraser commission recommended a series of measures aimed at widening participation and in response to it a number of states passed legislation requiring primaries to be held. There is no uniformity between the states: different rules govern who can vote in these contests. Moreover, it has been left to the parties to determine how the results are reflected in the nominating process.

In 2008, for example, the Republicans adopted a "winner-takes-all" system whereby the candidate with the most votes in each state congressional district received the support of all that district's delegates. That meant that the eventual nominee, John McCain, was able to build up the number of delegates committed to support him at the party convention by March 4 that year, when his victories in primaries in Ohio, Texas, Rhode Island and Vermont gave him an unassailable lead over his closest rival, Mick Huckabee. On the other hand, the Democrats opted for a more proportional system: delegates were allocated on the basis of the percentage votes cast for each candidate (subject to attaining a minimum of fifteen percent of the vote).

This had an impact on the outcome. In those states where Obama lost the primary election to Clinton, he still won some delegate support to take forward to the convention. California illustrates how the rules shaped the fortunes of rival candidates. On the Republican side, John McCain won 155 of the state's

170 delegates, despite gaining only forty-three percent of the statewide vote. His nearest rival, Mick Huckabee, received the remaining fifteen delegates although he had accumulated almost thirty-five percent of the vote. For the Democrats, on the other hand, Hillary Clinton grabbed the Californian headlines by winning the primary vote overall with almost fifty-two percent of the vote. But Barack Obama still emerged with 166 pledged delegates from the state compared with the 204 who supported his rival.

By the time the Democrats gathered for their national nominating convention in Denver in August 2008, therefore, the Obama campaign had proven its resilience together with its ability to gather support not only through caucuses and primaries but also among "super-delegates," those party members who had an automatic right to vote at the convention and whose ability to influence the outcome of the process had been an object of media speculation for months. The result of the nominating process was no longer in doubt. The Convention, like that of the Republicans which was held shortly afterwards, thus fulfilled the purpose that it now has assumed within the electoral process. Democrats and Republicans attempt to transcend rivalries within their parties. Political choreography is carefully stage managed. In Denver, Hillary Clinton's intervention to demand that the Convention nominate Obama by acclamation was an important symbolic gesture. The public reconciliation of former rivals allows the party's chosen candidates immediately to recalibrate their campaigns, engaging now with the American electorate rather than just the party faithful as the winning post of the White House comes into view. Yet the rules of the game are still significant: it is at this stage that the need to win a majority in the Electoral College rather than simply the popular vote determines not only strategies but also outcomes.

To win the White House, it is necessary to put together a winning coalition of states that can deliver a majority of votes in the Electoral College. While this preserves the influence of federalism in presidential elections – winning states is more important than winning the popular vote – historically it has had profound political repercussions. It has determined the party's choice of candidates and the electoral strategies they have employed. Initially the South's over-representation in Congress (where slaves were counted as three-fifths for apportionment purposes) gave the region an in-built advantage in the Electoral College as well. Before the Civil War, nine out of fifteen Presidents came from states that would join the Confederacy. In 1860, Lincoln's election was a watershed. He won without receiving a single Electoral College vote below the Mason-Dixon line that separated the slave-owning southern states from their northern free-labor neighbors. This demonstrated that the South's influence on the presidency had been progressively eroded by the growth of population in the north. In 1790, the populations of the two regions had been roughly equal. Sixty years later, there were seven million more people living in the North of the United States than in the South. Lincoln's emphatic victory in the Electoral College proved to the South that its capacity to influence federal politics and elections to the Executive had been irrevocably eroded and forced the final stages of the secession crisis that led to the outbreak of Civil War.

After 1865 Republicans continued to be able to win the White House without the support of the South in the Electoral College, where, once Reconstruction ended, "the party of Lincoln" could expect to gain few votes from the former Confederacy. The geographical heart of the party was in the Midwest, with Ohio in particular becoming the state from which the party's presidential candidates were drawn. Seven of the eleven Republicans who occupied the White House between 1868 and 1932 came from the state. By the time the Republicans re-captured the White House in 1952 its political center of gravity had moved westwards. In Dwight Eisenhower from

Kansas it found a candidate whose status as a war hero transcended specific sectional appeal, but his selection of his running mate was influenced in part by electoral considerations. The then Senator Richard Nixon was from California, a state which in that year for the first time had more votes in the Electoral College than Ohio. When Nixon finally managed to win the White House in 1968 it emphasized the importance of the West in the Republican's choice of candidate: an influence confirmed when the state's former Republican governor, Ronald Reagan, became President twelve years later.

On the other hand, after the Civil War, Democrats realized that they could not hope for an Electoral College majority without carrying the popular vote in some northern states. Between 1865 and 1912, Grover Cleveland from New York was the party's only successful presidential candidate. In that year, Woodrow Wilson, whose political career had been established in the North as Governor of New Jersey, became the first Democrat nominee since the Civil War to be born and raised in the former Confederacy. After Wilson, it was not until 1932 that another Democrat, Franklin Roosevelt, was successful in forging a coalition between northern and southern states that brought with it an Electoral College majority. Roosevelt too demonstrated the electoral advantages for the Democrats of nominating a northerner and a southerner to "balance the ticket." His running mate, John Nance Garner from Texas, became the first southerner to occupy an office in the federal Executive since the Civil War. In 1960, in selecting Lyndon Johnson, also from Texas, for the Vice-Presidency, John F. Kennedy followed Roosevelt's political wisdom in maximizing the geographical appeal of the Democrat ticket.

In 1964, Lyndon Johnson became the first southern Democrat to be elected President since the end of the Civil War. During his time in office, he changed the party and the electoral landscape of American politics. Southern Democrats who opposed

Johnson's support for Civil Rights found a new home within the Republican party. Within a generation, Johnson's home state of Texas had become a Republican stronghold and the state from which the then Governor, George W. Bush, would launch his successful bid for the White House. At the same time, after Johnson himself had demonstrated that a southern Democrat could win the presidency, the party's next two successful nominees, Jimmy Carter (Governor of Georgia) and Bill Clinton (Governor of Arkansas) both came from the South. Indeed, Clinton also rejected the tradition of balancing the ticket in selecting his fellow southerner, Al Gore from Tennessee, as his running mate.

Historically, then, there have been some states – and regions of the country – that over time have become dependable strongholds for either the Democrats or the Republicans in the Electoral College. The conventional political wisdom in the United States is that the outcome of each contest thus depends on a candidate's ability to win over a few marginal and critical "battleground states." In recent times, winning at least one of Ohio, Florida and Pennsylvania has been seen as critical to a campaign's eventual success. From time to time, however, the established jigsaw of the Electoral College has been overturned. In 1932, it was the onset of the Great Depression that helped Franklin Roosevelt to his landslide victory. He won the Electoral College vote by 472 to fifty-nine against the incumbent Herbert Hoover and carried forty-two of the fifty states. In 2008 the economic crisis that erupted during the latter stages of the campaign undoubtedly helped Barack Obama to win the White House. Yet his victory was also built upon his success in broadening participation and appealing to a new generation of voters who altered the political balance of power in a number of key states. Obama's campaign attracted some criticism for its strategy of competing for votes in those states that were considered to be Republican. Nevertheless it proved successful not only in increasing voter turnout but also in delivering Obama's convincing victory of 365 votes to 173 in the Electoral College.

The disintegration of the "solid south" that supported the Democrats after the Civil War has meant that in more recent times geographical concerns and home state Electoral College votes may have become less significant in determining the choice of vice-presidential nominees: in 2008, for example, Obama's running mate, Joe Biden, came from the small state of Delaware. Nevertheless the continued existence of the Electoral College remains an important influence on the electoral strategies that candidates for the White House pursue. So too is money. The ability to raise funds to support the enormous expenditure involved in the perpetual campaign is critical to electoral success. Moreover, the fact that money can bring with it crucial advantages in the capacity to build and sustain a viable challenge for political office means that campaign finance reform remains a persistent and controversial issue in American politics.

Follow the money

On January 21, 2010 the Supreme Court issued its decision in the case of *Citizens United v. Federal Election Commission*. It had been brought under the provisions of the Campaign Reform Act of 2002 (popularly known as the McCain-Feingold Act after its co-sponsors in the Senate). Citizens United had been barred from placing television advertisements for a documentary film critical of Hillary Clinton's role in the scandals that had punctuated her husband's time in the White House, which it released during the 2008 primary season. According to its website, it is "an organization dedicated to restoring our government to citizens' control." Its "goal is to restore the founding fathers' vision of a free nation, guided by the honesty, common sense, and good will of its citizens." Such laudable aims nevertheless suggest a conservative Republican perspective that suffused its anti-Clinton documentary.

Citizens United fought the ban on advertising its documentary on the grounds that it infringed first amendment rights to freedom of speech. The Supreme Court agreed. In a five to four decision the Court ruled that: "Because speech is an essential mechanism of democracy – it is the means to hold officials accountable to the people – political speech must prevail against laws that would suppress it by design or inadvertence." To its critics, however, the Court's decision effectively lifted any restrictions on major corporations and labor unions now funding political advertising: one of the key objectives of the McCain-Feingold Act. Seven days later, in his State of the Union Address, President Obama was highly critical of the decision, suggesting that:

> With all due deference to separation of powers, last week the Supreme Court reversed a century of law that I believe will open the floodgates for special interests – including foreign corporations – to spend without limit in our elections. I don't think American elections should be bankrolled by America's most powerful interests, or worse, by foreign entities. They should be decided by the American people. And I'd urge Democrats and Republicans to pass a bill that helps to correct some of these problems.

Among the Supreme Court Justices gathered in Congress to hear the President's speech, Samuel Alito was seen to shake his head in disapproval of Obama's words: a dramatic illustration of how the Executive and the Judiciary can find themselves at odds on a controversial political issue.

Finance in an era of the perpetual campaign remains a perennial political problem. Candidates need cash. Raising money to run for office is a central part of political activity in the United States. Despite attempts such as McCain-Feingold to limit the capacity of special interest groups to attempt to influence the political process through campaign donations, money is still the political drug of choice and necessity for any American politician to have a realistic chance of winning an election for federal or state office. The Obama campaign illustrates the point. Its unprecedented fundraising ability enabled it to compete with Hillary Clinton throughout the primary season. By declining public funding that would have limited his expenditure during his election battle with John McCain, moreover, the Democrat candidate was able to comprehensively out-raise and out-spend his Republican rival. Obama benefited from $750 million in campaign donations. In contrast, McCain could only muster $370 million in campaign contributions: a little less than half as much.

Since the influential Republican Senator from Ohio, Mark Hanna, responded to the populist threat of the Democrat William Jennings Bryan in 1896 – by persuading wealthy sympathizers to donate money to the cause of electing William McKinley to the presidency – it has generally been the case that the candidate with the most funding wins. Moreover, the costs escalate with every electoral cycle. In 2000, the total spending by candidates for the presidency, the House of Representatives and the Senate was a little over $3 billion. Four years later it was $4 billion and in 2008 it had reached $5 billion, with $1 billion being invested in the campaigns of the two major candidates for the White House.

"Follow the money" was the advice that Mark Felt, the source eventually revealed as "Deep Throat," gave to the *Washington Post* investigative reporter Bob Woodward at the time of the Watergate scandal. In 1971, President Richard Nixon had signed the Federal Election Campaign Act into law. What was revealed shortly afterwards was the ability of an incumbent President to raise money covertly to facilitate a re-election campaign. Nixon's complicity was only revealed after arrests were made during the break-in at the Democrat's campaign headquarters in the Watergate building. The crimes of Watergate dramatized the extent of Nixon's non-compliance with the provisions of the act. It had attempted to limit the campaign contributions made by individuals and organizations such as political action committees (PACs), groups set up to support a candidate for election. The Federal Election Campaign Act had required more stringent disclosure of the amounts being donated and the purposes to which the money was put. With no capacity to enforce its provisions, however, the measures were easily ignored, as Nixon's behavior demonstrated. In the aftermath of his resignation, therefore, Congress amended the act, creating the Federal Election Commission as an independent agency to police its provisions. Public funding for presidential elections was introduced in time for the 1976 campaign. In the same year, however, the Supreme Court decided in the case of *Buckley v. Valeo* that while limits on contributions should be restricted, limits on expenditures were an unconstitutional violation of free speech – the argument that it would return to in its 2010 decision in favor of Citizens United.

The McCain-Feingold Act in 2002 was passed as an admission that previous attempts at campaign finance reform had not resolved the problems surrounding the issue. Or rather, it acknowledged the fact that, given the importance of money in the electoral process, any reform was likely to result in new and creative ways of circumventing the law. The act prohibited political parties from raising and spending so-called "soft money," not subject to federal limits, in support of a candidate's individual campaign. It also sought to limit the number of advertisements that purported to be addressing issues and which were broadcast in the immediate run-up to an election by defining them as "electioneering communications" if they named the candidate and prohibiting them if they were paid for by a corporation. It was this provision that in 2010 once more drew the Supreme

Court into the political fray. When President Obama voiced his criticism of the Court's decision he was echoing a widespread concern among politicians and voters alike. John McCain, his defeated opponent in the 2008 election, observed that Supreme Court Justices "have no experience in the political area" and predicted that "we are now going to see an inundation of special-interest money into political campaigns" which would lessen "the influence of average citizens." The former sponsor of the measure to which he gave his name now thought that the entire issue of campaign finance reform was "dead." Following the President's State of the Union Address, an *ABC News/Washington Post* poll found that eighty percent of those asked opposed the Court's decision, with sixty-five percent registering "strong" dis-approval. Yet legislation proposed to reinstate some of the limits on corporate campaign spending stalled in Congress and cam-paign finance reform lost traction among voters as an issue during the 2010 mid-term elections.

The fact that it has proven so difficult to achieve comprehen-sive campaign finance reform has as much to do with the ever increasing expense of running for office in the United States as it has to do with the political in-fighting that surrounds the issue. The competitive advantage that money brings in enabling candidates to buy advertising space and time in key media markets across America is so sought after that those who are most successful in raising funds are reluctant to surrender it and fight instead on a more level financial playing field. In the market-place of American politics the costs of joining the race mean that the barriers to entry for candidates not sponsored by the two major parties may be prohibitive. In 1992, the quixotic campaign of the diminutive Texan billionaire Ross Perot for the presidency was a personally financed crusade that proved to be more suc-cessful than most (for a while he even led in the polls), and ended with him gaining almost nineteen percent of the national vote, but no Electoral College votes. Even major party candidates –

Hillary Clinton is a recent example – have committed some of their personal wealth to their campaigns for the party nomination. Money is a key to success and the urge to gamble is strong – as is the constant temptation to find ways to maximize income within (or, as Nixon demonstrated, outside) the prevailing and ever changing rules of the game.

Elections and the party system

Competitive elections are central to the idea of a democratic republic that rests on the principle of popular sovereignty. Despite the philosophical objections shared by many of the founders that political parties were a bad idea, it was ultimately apparent that the United States could not function without them. The first Congress had barely assembled before first Hamilton and then Jefferson (along with Madison) started to organize in order to gather support for their policies within the Legislature and to try to win a majority there through successful campaigning at the polls. During the first federal Congress, within the House of Representatives, almost seventy percent of members could be relied upon to support Washington's administration (in effect the stirrings of the Hamiltonian Federalist party). The Senate was less secure, with thirty-six Senators consistently voting with the administration and twenty-eight against. After the first mid-term elections, however, the House of Representatives was more evenly divided and in the Senate the administration struggled to win a majority: an early indication of the subsequent and often frequent electoral setbacks that may erode a President's influence within the Legislature.

As the "era of good feelings" soured, the collapse of party competition that had occurred after Jefferson's election in 1800 proved to be but a temporary suspension of political hostilities. Thereafter the Democrats and, following the Civil War, the

Republicans established themselves in the United States as the only parties capable of electing candidates to the White House and as rivals for control of the federal Legislature. Their ideological principles proved adaptable as they sought electoral advantage. Indeed, it is the demands of the perpetual campaign that nowadays shape their political outlooks. Every four years the party that fails to win the presidency can still hope to have a majority in one or both houses of the Legislature. If it does not manage to achieve that ambition, it has only to wait two years until mid-term elections give it the opportunity to reverse its losses. In such circumstances it is easy for the opposition to ignore appeals for bi-partisan action in the national interest and instead do everything it can to frustrate the President's agenda. Even those who come to office promising change – and President Obama is a recent example – find the political culture that exists on Capitol Hill a formidable obstacle to legislative achievement.

It may be, therefore, that the Founders' initial suspicions of political parties as a threat to republican democracy were well founded. Yet there is no alternative to them. In the United States, the Democrats and the Republicans have demonstrated a remarkable capacity to find fresh coalitions of supporters among the American electorate. At the same time it is important to remember that Democrats and Republicans organize for elections at the federal and the state level and campaign for public office for the Executive and the Legislature both nationally and locally. The apparent two-party juggernaut that dominates the nation's electoral process is, from another perspective, a kaleidoscope of different elements that focuses on a range of ambitions and objectives.

For the presidency it is the Electoral College that, for all its obscurity, is still a permanent feature of the electoral landscape. Putting together a coalition of states to win a majority there is the final challenge for those candidates who have successfully negotiated the obstacle course of the nomination process. Moreover, the ability to raise money is still the most important asset that a candidate can bring to the race. As technological advances make campaigning ever more sophisticated, the private space which separates those who aspire to public office from those whose support they need is becoming increasingly narrow. Nowadays, social networking and political networking use the same communication technologies. Email, Facebook and Twitter take their place beside speeches, debates and advertising as means by which candidates try to build support in their relentless pursuit of votes. It is but the latest development in the perpetual campaign that was set in motion over two hundred years ago as the first federal elections took place in the newly established United States of America.

4

State governments and the politics of federalism

Nowadays it seems inevitable that the American political spotlight is fixed on Washington DC. The federal government has assumed a central role as the President and Congress either cooperate or do battle in their attempts to put policy into action and to frame the nation's laws. Yet although the Constitution's preamble opens with the famous phrase "We the people," the contemporary reality cannot hide the historical fact that it was "we the States" which came together in 1787 to design what their representatives intended to be a federal republic. That meant there would be a division of power between the national and the state governments, the boundaries of which would be open to constant debate and redefinition. If, since the end of the Civil War, it has been the federal government whose influence has predominated in the nation's politics, the states still have an impact on the immediate lives of their citizens. The role that federalism still plays in the politics of the United States should be neither overlooked nor underestimated.

The introduction of progressive reforms within some states has resulted in more "direct democracy," giving their populations a say on matters of political, economic and social concern. Mapping the cultural geography of the United States suggests that regional political attitudes – in the states of the East and West coasts, the South and the Midwest – impact on contemporary issues such as gun control, crime and punishment, race, gay marriage and women's rights. While some states are progressive, others are reactionary. Nevertheless, through preserving the idea of federalism together they continue to make a significant contribution to the vitality and variety of political life in the United States of America.

States' rights or federal power?

Why did the original thirteen states agree to join the Union? The answer is given in the Constitution's opening lines. The committee that framed them, chaired by Gouverneur Morris from Pennsylvania, agreed unanimously that it was to "form a more perfect Union, establish Justice, insure domestic Tranquility, provide for the common defence, promote the general Welfare and secure the Blessings of Liberty to ourselves and our Posterity." Among these aims, at the time it was political stability within the United States and national security in the face of external threats that were paramount concerns. So the states were prepared to give up some political independence in the hope of securing the benefits which they were persuaded that they could gain from eventually signing up to Madison's plan.

In the Bill of Rights, the tenth and final amendment specifies that "the powers not delegated to the United States by the Constitution, nor prohibited by it to the States, are reserved to the States respectively, or to the people." From the start, however, it was evident that the federal government would test the limits of its constitutional power while the states would resist encroachments on what they saw as their legitimate spheres of authority. The first American political party system coalesced around this political division: the Federalists' vision of a strong central government versus the Democrat-Republican ideal of the national government remaining subservient to the states.

When states objected to the federal government's actions they discussed and sometimes tried to assert what they saw as their right to leave the Union. During the war of 1812, the British tried to isolate the New England states on the Atlantic seaboard from the rest of the United States. Connecticut, New Hampshire and Massachusetts remained on the sidelines of the conflict. In 1814 as the war impacted upon their economies, representatives from those states were joined by emissaries from Rhode Island and Vermont in Hartford, Connecticut, where the idea of secession was debated. The New England states decided to stay in the Union – and the end of the war pre-empted any further action. Nevertheless it was an indication that when political antagonisms flared the threat of disunion remained.

In 1828 the federal Congress agreed to impose a protective tariff designed to give northern industries an advantage against foreign competition. Its domestic impact was felt disproportionately in the South, as other nations retaliated against America's action. The market for its primary export – cotton – was affected, particularly in Britain, as a result of what southerners came to call the "Tariff of Abominations."

South Carolina challenged Washington over the issue in 1828 and again when another tariff measure was passed in 1832. Its legislature passed an Ordinance of Nullification which asserted that the state could ignore a federal law with which it disagreed. As President, Andrew Jackson argued that South Carolina's defiance was a direct threat to the idea of Union itself. In his "Proclamation to the People of South Carolina," he pointed out in no uncertain terms that:

> If this doctrine had been established at an earlier day, the Union would have been dissolved in its infancy … You must perceive

> that the crisis your conduct presents at this day would recur
> whenever any law of the United States displeased any of the
> States, and that we should soon cease to be a nation.

Jackson threatened to hang the leaders of the nullification
movement: an outcome that was avoided when Congress
managed to pass a compromise tariff that defused the constitutional crisis.

Compromise was indeed the key to the federal republic's
survival in the years following its establishment. When new
territories applied to join the Union, the controversy over the
expansion of slavery became a political issue that was resolved by
the federal government in Washington only through negotiated
agreements between northern and southern states. In 1820 and
1850, settlements that satisfied both North and South were
engineered by Henry Clay, the first of which proved more
durable than the second. As abolitionist sentiment grew in the
North, the assertion of states' rights in defense of slavery in the
South became a philosophical as well as a political imperative.
From South Carolina, John C. Calhoun, who had been a leading
advocate for the nullification doctrine, argued in his *Discourse on
the Constitution and Government of the United States*, published
posthumously in 1853, that:

> There is indeed no such community, *politically* speaking, as the
> people of the United States, regarded in the light of, and as con-
> stituting one people or nation … The whole, taken together,
> form a federal community: – a community composed of States
> united by a political compact; and not a nation composed of
> individuals united by what is called a social compact.

For Calhoun, it had been a fundamental error to begin the
preamble to the Constitution with its famous reference to
"we the people."

ABOLITIONISTS

The movement to abolish slavery in the United States gained momentum in the pre-Civil War period. In 1833, William Lloyd Garrison, editor of the *Liberator*, the abolitionist newspaper, formed the American Anti-Slavery Society to campaign for an end to the South's "peculiar institution." Leading abolitionists included the freed slave Frederick Douglass and Harriet Beecher Stowe, who published the influential anti-slavery novel *Uncle Tom's Cabin* (1852).

Instead, at a time when the South's influence in the federal Legislature and its capacity to win a majority in the Electoral College had been progressively weakened by the expansion of population in non-slave states, Calhoun argued the case for an assertive form of federalism. In his opinion:

> the choice lies between a national, consolidated and irresponsible government of a dominant portion or section of the country, – and a federal, constitutional and responsible government, with all the divisions of powers indispensable to form and preserve such a government in a country of vast extent, and so great a diversity of interests and institutions as ours.

Yet Calhoun was also a political realist. He saw that his advocacy of states' rights was irrevocably linked to the preservation of slavery. In his last speech to the Senate (read for him as he was by then too ill to deliver it himself), he derided the government of the United States, now dominated by a majority in the North, as having become "as absolute as that of the Autocrat of Russia, and as despotic in its tendency as any government that ever existed." He also predicted that in the end "the South will be forced to choose between abolition and secession."

As the United States hesitated before plunging from the constitutional precipice into Civil War, the principle of federalism
expressed in terms of states' rights defined the schism which, as
Calhoun saw, would end with those states which joined the
Confederacy making their decision to leave the Union. In 1858,
in his debates with Abraham Lincoln in Illinois as part of their
campaigns for the federal Senate, Stephen Douglas, another notable advocate for states' rights, argued that it should be left to the
people within each state – whether already in the Union or
applying for admission to it – to decide whether slavery should
be allowed within its borders. In his view, those who had drawn
up the Constitution had known that "in a country as wide and
broad as this, with such a variety of climate, production, and
interest, the people necessarily required different laws and institutions in different localities … [T]he laws and regulations which
would suit the granite hills of New Hampshire would be unsuited
to the rice-plantations of South Carolina." That indeed was the
essence of the federal idea, "that each State should retain its own
legislature and its own sovereignty, with the full and complete
power to do as it pleased within its own limits, in all that was
local and not national." The problem, however, was that the existence of slavery in the South and the prospect of its extension as
more territories were organized for statehood meant that federalism as a constitutional principle could not accommodate the
moral dimensions of the political debate over abolitionism.
Calhoun saw that. So too did Lincoln, who with characteristic
eloquence put the matter simply in his observation that "a house
divided against itself cannot stand."

Those who agreed with Calhoun and Douglas argued the
constitutional case for the states to be regarded as "separate and
equal" in their relationship with the federal government. Pressed
to the limit, however, states' rights led to the South's secession
from the Union. One reason the Civil War was fought was
to keep the United States united. Even though slavery was

LINCOLN–DOUGLAS DEBATES

As part of the campaign for the federal Senate in Illinois in 1858, Abraham Lincoln and Stephen Douglas took part in a series of seven debates throughout the state. Their subject was slavery: did states have the right to preserve and even extend it or should the federal government intervene to end it? Douglas, the incumbent Senator, advocated for states' rights. Lincoln argued that the United States could not continue half slave and half free. Lincoln lost the election but the debates brought him to national prominence and acted as his springboard to the White House two years later.

abolished in the South, however, when the states of the former Confederacy were finally brought back into the union, they were allowed to construct and maintain a system of racial separatism that lasted for almost a hundred years.

"New federalism"

During the twentieth century, Washington's constitutional responsibility to promote the nation's general welfare and common defense took on fresh relevance. The economic depression of the 1930s demanded a coordinated national response and federal government intervention in the shape of Franklin Roosevelt's New Deal. Moreover, America's increasingly central role on the world stage, notably after the Second World War and with the acquisition of a nuclear arsenal, meant that the states appeared progressively marginalized in the face of increasing federal power.

By the 1980s, many Americans had come to agree with Ronald Reagan, who, in his first inaugural address as President, proclaimed that "government is not the solution to our problem; government is the problem." He was referring specifically to the government located in the city in which he had just come to live: Washington DC. Reagan's view that the role of the federal government had ballooned out of proportion with the founder's original intent led him to support a re-assertion of the principle of federalism, devolving more power and responsibility to the states. In his memoirs he wrote of his time as Governor of California, when he had:

> experienced how the federal bureaucracy had its hand in everything … Washington would establish a new program that the states were supposed to administer, then set so many rules and regulations that the state wasn't really administering it – you were just following orders from Washington.

In his inaugural address, therefore, he signaled his intent "to curb the size and influence of the Federal establishment and to demand recognition of the distinction between the powers granted to the federal government and those reserved to the states or to the people." Reagan believed that the United States "had strayed a great distance from our founding fathers' vision of America." Aged twenty-one in 1932, his first vote had been for Franklin Roosevelt and the New Deal. But as a Republican governor in the 1960s when Lyndon Johnson was constructing his "Great Society," his suspicion of centralized government had been confirmed. Looking back over the time between LBJ's burst of federal government activism and his own election to the White House in 1980, Reagan concluded that the "myriad of new federal programs" had included hardly "any that did much good for the poor or the nation as a whole." The so-called "Reagan Revolution" represented the biggest change in the public philosophy of the United States for fifty years, and at its heart was the President's conviction that the states should be restored to their proper constitutional position in relation to the federal government.

In an Executive Order published on October 26, 1987, Reagan set out his understanding of the concept of federalism. Among several "fundamental federalism principles" he proclaimed that "the people of the States are free, subject only to restrictions in the Constitution itself or in constitutionally authorized Acts of Congress, to define the moral, political, and legal character of their lives." That language would have met with the approval of many in the pre-Civil War South, but in an America that had finally recognized the legitimacy of the case for Civil Rights (ironically through the actions of Lyndon Johnson, with whom Reagan had violently disagreed on most other political issues), the President was not seeking to defend the morally indefensible. Rather he argued that:

> policies of the national government should recognize the responsibility of – and should encourage opportunities for – individuals, families, neighborhoods, local governments, and private associations to achieve their personal, social, and economic objectives through cooperative effort.

Reagan's "new federalism" was part of his ambition to reduce the size of the national government and its expenditure by allowing individual states to pursue their own initiatives in areas of public policy that had previously been seen as Washington's preserve. This desire to rebalance the responsibilities of federal and state governments influenced the President's approach to a number of issues, notably in the area of welfare provision. In his first State of the Union Address in 1982, he announced that responsibility for administering Aid to Families with Dependent Children (a program of federal assistance whose origins dated to the New Deal era) and food stamps would be transferred to the states. The President was convinced that "this will make welfare less costly and more responsive to genuine need because it will be designed and administered closer to the grass roots and the people it serves." His plan, which was subsequently shelved as unworkable, involved a "welfare swap" by which the federal government was to take over the administration of Medicaid, a centerpiece of Lyndon Johnson's "Great Society" reforms during the 1960s.

Despite setbacks, the Reagan administration continued to press for welfare reform and found support from both Republican and Democrat state governors. In 1988, the President spoke to a number of them who had come to Washington to lobby for the Senate to pass a welfare reform bill. He took the opportunity to remind the governors of his view that it was the states that should take the initiative in dealing with such issues. He argued that "Perhaps the greatest test of federalism is how we meet the urgent need for welfare reform, how successful we are in fashioning the local and community solutions to problems that would destroy families." In his remarks on signing the Family Support Act of 1988 into law, Reagan pointed out that the welfare to work provisions in the measure were similar to those included in a state initiative passed while he was Governor of California. He also praised the reform efforts championed by the National Governors Association, mentioning by name the then Democrat Governor of Arkansas, Bill Clinton.

As President, in 1996, Clinton fulfilled the commitment he gave in his first State of the Union Address to "end welfare as we know it." His approach to achieving that ambition reflected his own experience as a state governor and his cooption of elements of Reagan's philosophy of "new federalism," particularly after the Republicans, under the leadership of Newt Gingrich in the House of Representatives and Bob Dole in the Senate, won convincing majorities in the 1994 mid-term congressional elections. The Clinton administration granted waivers from federal rules to over forty states to allow them to pursue their own strategies to reduce welfare dependency.

In states such as Wisconsin and Indiana, which were among the first to chart their own directions, the numbers on welfare were reduced dramatically. In August 1996 Clinton signed the Personal Responsibility and Work Opportunity Reconciliation Act that allowed states to shape reforms based on the needs of their own communities.

Clinton had famously proclaimed in his State of the Union Address earlier that year that "the era of big government is over ... our new, smaller government must work in an old-fashioned American way, together with all of our citizens through state and local governments, in the workplace, in religious, charitable and civic associations." If his language reflected Reagan's re-shaping of America's public philosophy, his approach to welfare reform similarly went a long way to meeting the former Republican President's belief in the continuing influence of federalism as the most critical force for change in American political life. Reagan's and Clinton's attitudes to federalism appeared to have much in common. However, Clinton's successor, George W. Bush, who also came to the White House after becoming a state governor, did not pursue "new federalism" with anything like the vigor of his predecessors. He appeared instead to be intent on an increase in federal authority rather than an expansion of states' rights, not least in the aftermath of the 9/11 attacks which defined the conduct of his administration. On certain issues, this prompted individual states to act in defiance of the federal administration and adopt policies that the President opposed. In 2002, for example, California's legislature approved a law to allow scientific research on embryonic stem cells. While Bush wanted to restrict money available for stem cell research, two years later, California's voters approved Proposition 71 which provided $3 billion funding for research in this area during the subsequent decade. Governor Arnold Schwarzenegger was among those who supported the proposition, expressing his disagreement with his fellow Republican in the White House.

On May 20, 2009, President Barack Obama issued a 'Memorandum for the Heads of Executive Departments and Agencies'. In it, he observed that:

> the Federal Government's role in promoting the general welfare and guarding individual liberties is critical but State law and national law often operate concurrently to provide independent safeguards for the public. Throughout our history, State and local governments have frequently protected health, safety and the environment more aggressively than has the national Government.

The new President was sympathetic to the idea of what his administration called "progressive federalism," seeking to co-operate with like-minded governors to achieve change in areas central to his political agenda. In his memorandum, Obama also reminded the departments and agencies of the Executive branch he headed that they "should be mindful that in our Federal system, the citizens of the several States have distinctive circum-stances and values, and that in many instances it is appropriate for them to apply to themselves rules and principles that reflect these circumstances and values." A commitment to the federal ideal entails an appreciation of the diversity of the United States.

Diversity in unity

Immigration and migration, patterns of settlement, historical development, economic circumstances, industrialization, urban-ization and religious sentiments are among the influences that have helped form the different characters of individual states. Even in colonial times political attitudes in the towns of Puritan New England could be contrasted with those of the slave-holding plantations in Virginia, Georgia and the Carolinas.

During the early part of the nineteenth century, moreover, as immigrants came to the United States from Europe, they fanned out across the continent to the new territories acquired through the Louisiana Purchase (1803). By 1840, the original thirteen states had doubled in number. The annexation of Texas (1845) and the war with Mexico (1846–1848) brought those areas of the former Hispanic empire in the Americas into the United States, broadening the ethnic mix of its population still further.

Once territories achieved a critical threshold of population, they could apply for statehood. This afforded fresh opportunities to consider how republican governments could be organized, and the new western states took the lead in adopting more open and democratic methods of doing political business. Consider California. In his fourth annual message to Congress in December 1848, President Polk observed that "it was known that mines of the precious metals existed to a considerable extent in California at the time of its acquisition." He went on to confirm that "The accounts of abundance of gold in that territory are of such an extraordinary character as would scarcely command belief … gold is found at various places in an extensive district of the country." He did not need to say any more. The rush for gold triggered such a rapid increase in population that two years later, in 1850, California was admitted to the Union as the first American state with a Pacific coastline. During the first half of that decade, indeed, the West coast state was responsible for just under half of the world's gold production, with its cities – notably San Francisco – booming as a result.

In 1849, California's state constitution was among the first to be put to a popular vote of the people living there, before it became part of the United States. Thirty years later, however, it was subjected to a radical overhaul as a result of widespread discontent with the political corruption that was then rife, the inequitable tax system and the conduct of – in particular – the railroad corporations in the state. At that time, there was also a widespread hostility directed against the Chinese who had settled on the West coast. Article Nineteen of the state's 1879 Constitution therefore prohibited any Californian corporation from hiring Chinese workers, barred them from any public sector employment and mandated the Legislature to "discourage their immigration by all the means within its power." The provision remained until 1952, when a number of amendments to the state constitution were put to a popular vote. Presenting the argument in favor of the Article's repeal, Thomas Maloney, the temporary speaker of the Assembly at the time, wrote: "To allow Article 19 to stand in the Constitution of the great state of California is to allow an antiquated and outmoded piece of legislation to adversely affect the dignity and prestige of our state." By then it had become more a reminder of California's past than relevant to its present.

At the time, the 1879 Constitution was seen as a populist revolt against the concentration of political and economic power in the hands of those who were unrepresentative of California's ordinary citizens, as well as an expression of nativist sentiment against immigrants from China. Lord Bryce, the British Liberal politician who was later to become Ambassador to the United States, wrote in *The American Commonwealth* (1889) that it was "an attempt to remedy the evils of the times by an attack in the shape of constitutional legislation upon wealth, and the various laws and systems by which wealth is accumulated and kept together." However, after visiting the West coast and observing the impact of the new Constitution, Bryce concluded that:

> the net result … was to give the monied classes in California a fright; to win for the State a bad name throughout America, and, by checking for a time the influx of capital, to retard her growth just when prosperity was reviving over the rest of the country.

In the end the new Constitution did little to change the prevailing distribution of political and economic power in the state. Nevertheless, California's hostility to the Chinese who had come to America was reflected at the national level when in 1882 the federal government passed the Chinese Exclusion Act. This was the first important federal law to restrict immigration to the United States.

Despite the limited success of its attempt to alter the political landscape through constitutional change, California had established a reputation as a state in which such popular insurgencies demanding reform became not only part of its heritage but also an illustration of the contemporary dynamics of its political life. Almost a century after it tore up its constitution, in 1978 a popular vote passed its famous Proposition 13, which made radical cuts (up to fifty percent) in property taxes in the state. More Californians participated in making that decision than voted in the election that renewed Jerry Brown's term as Governor held on the same day. Proposition 13 was the product of a campaign which took its case directly to the people of California rather than seeking to pass a law in the state legislature. It would not have been possible to do this in every other state: California, however, is among those states that have adopted a number of practices aimed at balancing the principles of representative and direct democracy.

In the early twentieth century, populist movements of the kind that had led to constitutional reform in California three decades earlier influenced progressive politicians to advocate for greater democratic accountability across the United States. This resulted in the adoption at state level of several practices intended to make government more responsive to the concerns of ordinary citizens by allowing balloting to take place on matters of public concern. Chief among these was the provision to allow petitions to be raised in favor of a legislative initiative or an amendment of the state constitution. An agreed threshold of popular support is needed before such proposals can be included in a ballot of the state's population. The referendum became a popular method of allowing a statewide vote on whether or not to repeal a specific legislative act (again a threshold of signatures needs to be reached before the referendum can be included on the ballot). Alternatively a state legislature may take the initiative in requiring a popular vote – another form of referendum – on proposed legislation.

Progressive reforms also became personal with the introduction of the provision in many states that elected officials could be removed from office through the practice of recall, whereby if a specified number of citizens demand it, a statewide vote then determines the fate of those whom they think are unfit for public office. In 1921, in North Dakota, Lynn Frazier became the first governor to be recalled: an economic depression in the state's agricultural sector led to political discontent. Eighty-two years later, Governor Gray Davis of California was recalled and replaced by Governor Arnold Schwarzenegger. Western states led the charge in adopting all or some of such practices and similar reforms spread across the United States as well, although the East coast states (with the exception of Vermont) remained largely immune to such changes.

Nevertheless, measures that receive widespread popular support within one state can start a band-wagon effect elsewhere. California's Proposition 13 was imitated in a number of other states and opposition to increased taxation found expression at the federal level with the election of Ronald Reagan to the White House shortly after its success in his home state. However, while involving ordinary citizens in proposing a legislative initiative, demanding a referendum or deciding whether a public official should be recalled undoubtedly increases political participation, there still remains an inherent tension between direct and representative democracy. The "taxpayers revolt" has meant that the state legislature is limited in its capacity to raise revenues and during economic recessions – such as that which impacted severely on California in 2008 – this has led to severe cuts in public sector budgets for education, welfare and the maintenance of the state's infrastructure. In recent years there has been renewed impetus to such populist methods of achieving political change. Statewide balloting on a variety of proposals, many of them involving moral concerns, has now become a familiar tactic for those, not least on the conservative right, who use legislative initiatives and demands for a referendum to advance their political agendas in the face of state legislatures which are often reluctant and unwilling to take up such controversial issues.

States of mind

States disagree. There are differences between them in the laws that govern those who live within their borders. Federal laws and state laws also coexist, sometimes in disharmony with one another. On issues such as gun control, capital punishment, as well as attitudes toward race, sexuality, women's rights, drug use and euthanasia, states retain jealously guarded rights that enable them to frame their own laws. While there are broad similarities in the way most states approach these issues, there are also significant differences that reflect the cultural and political geography of the nation.

Only California, Iowa, Maryland, Minnesota, New Jersey and New York do not have written into their state constitutions language that mirrors the sentiments of the second amendment with respect to the right to bear arms. Indeed, as the issue of gun control became increasingly controversial, some states added such sentiments in what were in some cases historic documents. For example, in 1987, following pressure from the state sportsmen's association, Delaware, the first state to join the Union, added a constitutional provision proclaiming that "a person has the right to keep and bear arms for the defense of self, family, home and State, and for hunting and recreational use." In some states the right to bear arms is linked specifically to the maintenance of a state militia. Hawaii, the last state to enter the union, has both an organized militia and also what its state law terms an "unorganized militia," whose members "are not members of national guard, the naval militia, or the state defense force." In 1978, when it amended its 1949 constitution to include the right to bear arms, it was thus able to incorporate the second amendment word for word.

State laws aimed at gun control coexist alongside federal provisions and in many cases are less restrictive locally than is the case at national level. In many states permits are not required in order to buy guns, although some states do insist on them for the purchase of machine guns or assault weapons. The powerful National Rifle Association (NRA), which is well organized as a political force at state level, has supported the "right to carry" weapons. In all but two states – Illinois and Wisconsin – laws have been passed that allow the carrying of concealed handguns. The NRA also uses its leverage, particularly in terms of its capacity to deliver electoral support for candidates who endorse its agenda, in state and federal elections. The outcome is that national gun control measures are difficult to pass and enforce in the face of opposition within the states. At the federal level, the Supreme Court has also supported a broad interpretation of the second amendment that does little to limit the ownership of guns. In the case of *District of Columbia v. Heller* (2008), it affirmed an individual's right to own guns for private use in federal enclaves such as Washington DC. Two years later, in *McDonald v. Chicago* (2010), the Court decided that the right to bear arms should be recognized by individual states as well.

At present, capital punishment is used in thirty-five of the fifty states. Regional attitudes toward this issue are becoming markedly different. The states which no longer have the death penalty are all on the East coast or in the Midwest of the continental United States (and Alaska and Hawaii are also among those states which do not sanction capital punishment). Michigan, Rhode Island and Wisconsin abolished it in the nineteenth century and other states followed at various times throughout the twentieth century. In New York, which held the first execution by means of the electric chair in 1890, the Court of Appeal decided in 2004 that the state's capital punishment statute was unconstitutional.

With the exception of West Virginia, southern states retain the death penalty. America's West also favors execution for capital offenses. Only North Dakota (since 1973) and New Mexico (since 2009) no longer have the death penalty. When New Mexico repealed its law there were only two inmates remaining on the state's "death row." In that same year, however, there were a total of 3,729 prisoners across the United States who had been convicted of capital crimes and were awaiting execution. California with almost 700 on its death row, Florida with 403 and Texas with 342 accounted for almost half the death row total. During the year, there were twenty-four executions carried out in Texas and another twenty-eight in ten other states.

These statistics show that while some states have comparatively high numbers among those sentenced to death, the rate of actual executions – apart from in Texas – is low. In 2009 only two sentences were carried out in Florida and none in California. Those convicted of capital crimes are spending an increasing time on death row: currently the average is over twelve years. Within states, the retention or abolition of the death penalty remains a divisive political issue that is dramatized whenever legal processes are exhausted, appeals for clemency rejected and an execution takes place. The variety of methods used in different states to carry out the death penalty has given rise to claims that the Bill of Rights' prohibition of "cruel and unusual punishments" may be infringed. Most states sanction the use of lethal injection but other methods – the electric chair, the gas chamber and hanging – still exist, as does the firing squad (which may be selected by those facing execution in Utah).

Although the death penalty also exists for certain federal crimes (the most recent execution was that of Timothy McVeigh six years after the 1995 bombing of the Alfred P. Murrah Federal Building in Oklahoma City), the history of capital punishment in America is thus firmly associated with the prevailing attitudes and practices adopted within individual states. Both have changed over time, but those who advocate for the abolition of capital punishment must continue to press their case on a state by state basis.

Nevertheless, the federal government has involved itself in this controversy. In 1972, the Supreme Court, ruling in *Furman v. Georgia*, agreed that the application of the death penalty was a "cruel and unusual punishment" that violated the eighth amendment of the Bill of Rights. The decision meant that in forty states death penalty statutes were unconstitutional. However, thirty-five states simply rewrote their laws to accommodate them to the Supreme Court's decision. These new statutes established a legal procedure for cases that involved capital punishment. Juries are now required to come to a verdict as to whether the defendant in a case is guilty of murder. Then, fresh evidence is introduced to establish whether the death penalty is the appropriate punishment. Juries are to be given guidance to help them reach a decision. The Supreme Court revisited the issue in 1976 in the case of *Gregg v. Georgia*, and upheld its earlier decision requiring these new procedures. In 1977, Gary Gilmour faced a firing squad in Utah and his execution marked the resumption of capital punishment in those states across America in which it was still sanctioned.

Although a racial minority in terms of the overall population of the United States, blacks are over-represented as a proportion of inmates on death row in most states. In 2009, in seven of the eleven states that prior to 1865 belonged to the former Confederacy, the number of blacks exceeded the number of whites awaiting execution for capital crimes. Of the other four states, only in Florida was the racial profile of death row more a reflection of national demographics (142 blacks and 222 whites). In Alabama, whites outnumbered blacks by four, in Georgia by two and in Tennessee by seven. Across the United States as a whole, prison populations are disproportionately composed of members of racial minorities. The legacy of the southern racial divide lingers still in the region's death rows.

Indeed, the issue of race has consistently permeated southern social attitudes. The so-called "Jim Crow" laws (the name itself was a racial slur directed toward African-Americans) were designed to keep the races apart in a structured system of discrimination and segregation. In 1961, when Barack Obama was born, his parent's marriage, which took place in Hawaii, would have been illegal in seventeen southern states, which still had anti-miscegenation laws in force. It was not only in the South that mixed race marriages were against state laws. In the West, California prohibited marriages between whites and Asians until 1948, while in other states such a ban remained in force for almost two more decades.

JIM CROW LAWS

Jim Crow was the name given to laws which enforced segregation in many American states for almost a century after the end of the Civil War. Separate hospitals, schools, restaurants and other public facilities were maintained and African-Americans experienced profound discrimination as a result. It took Supreme Court action, supported by the Civil Rights movement, to eventually dismantle these laws.

States were obliged to change their statutes preventing mixed marriages after the Supreme Court ruled, in the aptly named case of *Virginia v. Loving* (1967), in favor of Richard and Mildred Loving, a mixed race couple who had married in Washington DC but who were prevented from living as a married couple under the laws of their home state of Virginia. In its decision, the Court proclaimed that:

> Marriage is one of the "basic civil rights of man," fundamental to our very existence and survival … To deny this fundamental freedom on so unsupportable a basis as the racial classifications embodied in these statutes, classifications so directly subversive of the principle of equality at the heart of the Fourteenth Amendment, is surely to deprive all the State's citizens of liberty without due process of law. The Fourteenth Amendment requires that the freedom of choice to marry not be restricted by invidious racial discriminations. Under our Constitution, the freedom to marry, or not to marry, a person of another race resides with the individual and cannot be infringed by the State.

States gradually acceded to the Court's ruling and the ban became legally unenforceable. Nevertheless it took time to remove language prohibiting inter-racial marriage from state constitutions. In 1998, South Carolina, the first state to secede from the Union, amended its constitution to this effect, thirty-one years after the Court's ruling. It was not until the first year of the twenty-first century that the last state came into line when voters in an Alabama referendum approved the removal of this legacy of segregation from the state constitution.

Tolerance toward mixed race marriages across the nation has not been mirrored by widespread acceptance of same sex unions except in a handful of more liberal states. The federal government does not recognize same-sex unions – indeed, the "Defense of

Marriage Act," passed in 1996, defined marriage in relation to federal law as "only a legal union between one man and one woman as husband and wife." In signing the measure into law, the then President, Bill Clinton, nevertheless observed that "the Act confirms the right of each state to determine its own policy with respect to same gender marriage and clarifies for purposes of federal law the operative meaning of the terms 'marriage' and 'spouse'." Some states, therefore, have taken a different view on this issue and have been in the vanguard of social change. In 2010, five states – New Hampshire, Iowa, Massachusetts, Vermont and Connecticut (and also Washington DC) permitted same sex marriages.

In California, which from the 1960s onward had been at the forefront of the movement for greater toleration in social attitudes toward homosexuality, this issue continues to generate political controversy. After the state supreme court ruled in May 2008 that California's ban on same sex marriage was unconstitutional, "Proposition 8," included on the ballot in the November elections of that year, re-imposed the prohibition. Despite subsequent legal challenges, California now recognizes only those marriages which took place in the six months between June 2008 (when the state supreme court's decision went into effect) and November, when "Proposition 8" became law. The result of the ballot – fifty-two percent in favor and forty-eight percent opposed – shows that the issue remains a fault-line in contemporary Californian politics. In 2010 the ban was overturned in the courts, but the legal battles over the issue continue.

Attitudes toward abortion are even more controversial. In 1973, the Supreme Court's decision in *Roe v. Wade* invalidated many state and federal restrictions on whether and when a pregnancy could be terminated. While women's rights advocates hailed it as supporting the "right to choose," opponents of the decision mounted a sustained and often bitter campaign in defense of the "right to life." Their efforts at state level have resulted in a labyrinth of legislation that regulates and limits the circumstances in which terminations are legally allowed. All but twelve states insist that the procedure is carried out by a licensed physician and only allow it to take place after a defined period of time if a woman's health or indeed life is at risk. Just under half the states require a defined time to elapse between an initial consultation and the termination taking place. In thirty-four states, if the mother is not legally adult, there are specific requirements that mean parents must be involved in the decision. Thirty years after the Supreme Court's decision, a nationwide poll conducted by CBS news and the *New York Times* found some significant regional variations in social attitudes toward abortion. Whereas in the West of the country, eight-four percent of those asked thought that terminations should be permitted and in the Northeast eight-one percent agreed, in the South and Midwest only seventy-five percent thought abortion should be legal.

Despite federal prohibitions, laws relating to drug use also vary in states across the nation. In 1996, California passed "Proposition 215" which legalized the medical use of marijuana in defiance of the federal law which proscribed the drug from being used for any purpose. The federal ban was reinforced by the Supreme Court's ruling in the case of *Gonzales v. Raich* (2005). Nevertheless California still operates in defiance of federal law and has been joined by twelve other states that currently permit marijuana for medical use. In March 2009, Eric Holder, President Obama's attorney-general, announced that the federal government's policy would now be "to go after those people who violate both federal and state law," effectively admitting that the new administration would tolerate the fact that some states have partially decriminalized using the drug for medical purposes.

In 1994, a citizens' initiative in Oregon proposed a "Death with Dignity" measure to allow medically assisted suicide. It was agreed by a narrow margin and was subject to legal challenge in the courts. The state legislature tried to repeal it, and in 1997 called for a second vote on the measure which this time passed with an emphatic majority (sixty percent to forty percent). Oregon's act allows residents of the state who are terminally ill "to end their lives through the voluntary self-administration of lethal medications, expressly prescribed by a physician for that purpose." Voters in Michigan (1998) and Maine (2000) did not support similar initiatives in their states.

It remains a controversial issue. In 2008, just over a decade after Oregon finally approved its measure, voters in neighboring Washington State supported physician assisted suicide for residents who chose to exercise that right and who had less than six months to live. While campaigning for the presidency that year, Barack Obama said that he "thought that the people of Oregon did a service for the country in recognizing that as the population gets older we've got to think about issues of end-of-life care," while falling short of fully endorsing the state's position on assisted suicide. Nor did he comment on the move to adopt a similar "Death with Dignity" Act in Washington State. In keeping with his approach toward "new federalism," Obama was equally reticent in arguing for federal uniformity in those instances where clear majorities of a state's population indicated they were in favor of social policies that were not accepted across the nation.

The changing face of federalism

Federalism – the division of powers between the states and the national government – remains the beating heart of American constitutionalism. The balance that is struck between these two distinct and sometimes competing levels of authority is ever-changing. Historically the issue of states' rights was inextricably connected with the persistence of slavery: abolitionists channeled their efforts through the institutions of the federal government as the Southern states argued that the constitutional settlement of 1787 allowed them to preserve their "peculiar institution." Ultimately it was the defiance of the South and its secession from the Union which provoked the Civil War. During the twentieth century, the collapse of the national economy, America's involvement in the Second World War and its subsequent development as a "superpower" focused the political spotlight on Washington DC rather than the state capitals. But the change in public philosophy ushered in by the "Reagan Revolution" marked the contemporary beginnings of "new federalism": a re-balancing of the relationship between the federal and the state governments.

The United States has historically been a nation on the move. During the nineteenth century in particular, immigrants who came first to the Northeastern seaboard of the country fanned out across the continent, moving to the South, the Midwest and then on to the Pacific coast. Migration across the country has been an important influence in shaping contemporary American life, drawing people to different regions where clusters of states encompass distinctive political and social attitudes. Economic booms – and busts – have been driving forces in encouraging such mobility: the gold and land rushes in California and Oklahoma, for example, acted as magnets for migrants.

Then in the 1930s the Depression and the "dust bowl," the devastation caused by a succession of violent storms across the prairies, forced many to leave Oklahoma for California. Their journey, the inspiration for John Steinbeck's novel, *The Grapes of Wrath* (1939), represented one of the largest displacements of Americans from one area of the country in the nation's history. It took place over a shorter time span than the "Great Migration" of African-Americans away from the South that occurred throughout most of the twentieth century. Both these population shifts impacted on the politics of the states that were left behind and those where the migrants settled.

Oklahoma, for example, was one of the last states on the American continent to enter the Union, achieving statehood in 1907. William Jennings Bryan, the champion of the populist movement, told those meeting to frame its constitution that "It will be your own fault if you do not frame the best constitution ever written." The eventual document was notable not only for its length but also for the fact that it was heavily influenced by the progressive politics of the era. It established the popular election of all officeholders and provisions for both initiatives and a referendum on issues of statewide concern. However, the state's political allegiances have also been shaped by its proximity to its southern neighbors. Until the political re-alignment of the 1960s, following the passage of the Civil Rights Act, Oklahoma could be counted as part of the conservative Democrat "solid South" – indeed Lyndon Johnson was the last Democrat to carry the state in a presidential election.

Those who went west during the 1930s took their political attitudes with them. As they assimilated into Californian culture, they influenced the contemporary culture of the central valley region of the state where many of them settled. Patriotic and with a strong sense of individualism, their core values remained conservative, as reflected in their southern Baptist religious beliefs. This area remains as a political counter-weight to the liberalism of California's urban communities, notably in the cities of Los Angeles and San Francisco. For example, in the 2004 presidential election, John Kerry won a clear victory in Los Angeles, but in San Joaquin County, where many "Okies" had originally settled, there were more votes for George W. Bush. In 2008, whereas Barack Obama won just over eighty-four percent of San Francisco's vote, he had a victory margin of only ten percent over John McCain in San Joaquin County.

As African-Americans migrated from the South in the century after the end of the Civil War, black communities became established in cities in the North, Midwest and West. Between 1870 and 1890, Chicago's population of African-Americans almost quadrupled in size. By 1910 it had more than doubled again with most of the 40,000 blacks who had now settled there living in the South Side of the city. African-Americans continued to move to Chicago: another 50,000 came in the decade between 1910 and 1920, increasing racial tensions in the city as it struggled to absorb the new migrants. Housing shortages and competition for jobs in heavily unionized industries which discriminated against the newcomers helped provoke a race riot in 1919 in which twenty-three blacks died. After the Second World War a fresh wave of migration from the South meant that by the 1960s over three-quarters of a million African-Americans lived in Chicago and the city's South Side was widely regarded as the "black capital of America."

The impact on city – and state – politics was profound. Mayor Richard Daley, whose personal and political roots lay in the South Side Irish-American community, took office in 1955 and built Chicago's Democrat party machine into one of the most formidable forces in American urban politics. Following his death in office in 1976, his successors struggled to keep the Democrat machine intact and in 1983, supported by the votes of the South Side's black community, Harold Washington captured the party nomination and won election as Chicago's first African-American mayor.

Oscar Stanton De Priest, the son of former slaves and originally from Alabama, moved to Chicago in 1889 at the age of eighteen, and thirty years later became the first African-American to be elected to Congress in the twentieth century as a member of the federal House of Representatives. Blacks became active in city, state and federal politics. It is unsurprising, therefore, that in the 1990s a former community organizer on Chicago's South Side, who later married into a family originally from the slave state of South Carolina, should return from Harvard Law School to embark upon a political career that would lead him in twelve years from the Illinois State Senate to the White House. The personal stories of both Barack and Michelle Obama encapsulate the larger narrative of the "Great Migration" and its impact on American political culture.

President Obama's May 2009 memorandum to the Executive branch quoted an observation made by Louis Brandeis during the 1930s that "it is one of the happy accidents of the federal system that a single courageous state may, if its citizens choose, serve as a laboratory; and try novel social and economic experiments without risk to the rest of the country." Historically, the argument of the South, that the principle of states' rights justified the social and economic arrangements of slavery, helped to provoke the Civil War. Yet the contemporary diversity of America's fifty states remains a confirmation of the significant role that the federal ideal continues to play in the nation's political life.

5

Religion in American politics: "In God we trust"

In 1620, a group of Puritans left Plymouth in England for the colony they founded with the same name in New England. From the moment that they sailed up to Plymouth Rock, religion has been a touchstone of American cultural and political development. The still-celebrated voyage of the *Mayflower* was a pilgrimage in search of religious freedom but it had political significance as well. While crossing the Atlantic, the Puritans established the "covenant" or "compact" outlining principles for the government of the colony they hoped to establish in America. Subsequently regarded as a stepping stone toward the written constitution which established a federal government in the United States, the compact was seen as an example of the Puritans' political prescience in creating the structures of government necessary to the establishment of civil society in America.

MAYFLOWER COMPACT

The Mayflower Compact was drawn up during the Puritans' voyage to America. It established the rules by which their new colony was to be governed. It subsequently gained symbolic significance as a written constitution which was based on the principles of self-government: a model to be followed during and after the American War of Independence.

The influence of religion remains pervasive in American society which, even though it separates church and state, is nowadays far less secular than many European nations. The first amendment to the Constitution establishes freedom of religion, including the freedom not to profess a faith. But visitors to the United States may be struck by the number of churches of different denominations that are a characteristic feature of cities and towns across the country. Moreover, surveys consistently show that attendance at church is both widespread and common among Americans who adhere to and express their religious beliefs to a far greater extent than is the case in other developed nations. Yet there are inherent political tensions in a society founded on the philosophical principles of the enlightenment where many still seek to promote moral convictions and cultural beliefs shaped by their religious values.

The journalist H.L. Mencken famously defined Puritanism as "the haunting fear that someone, somewhere, may be happy." Nevertheless, the strict code of moral conduct insisted upon in Puritan communities suggests a continuing role for religion in American society. Republican democracy based on the principles of equality and liberty frees Americans from the hierarchies of social class and conduct that remained in many European nations – not least Britain – after feudalism disintegrated. However, if Jefferson's inalienable rights of "life, liberty and the pursuit of happiness" mean that individuals are entitled to behave and act in whatever manner they choose, irrespective of the potential offense they might give to others, then social harmony is threatened. To avoid such anarchy, individual liberty is best exercised within the limits of the agreed frameworks of morality that are the products of religious beliefs. Religion thus has an important role in establishing social cohesion: establishing an agreed sphere of individual liberty alongside the legitimate boundaries of public authority.

When the *Mayflower* finally dropped anchor in what is now Provincetown Harbor on Cape Cod, in contrast to the Europe they had left behind, the settlers on board found themselves in a world of abundance. The fish after which the cape was named could be caught simply by lowering a basket into the sea. They reported that salmon were also found in "prodigious quantities" along with other fish that were "so numerous that it is hazardous for Canoes" trying to navigate the Atlantic waters. On land, there were the crops already being cultivated by Native Americans: corn and "beans of various colors." This, then, was the promise of American life. The year after the *Mayflower* arrived, Edward Winslow, in his *Journal of the Pilgrims at Plymouth*, gave an account of the menu at the first Thanksgiving meal, held after the harvest had been gathered. "As much fowl" had been slaughtered "as, with a little help beside, served the company almost a week." The colonists "entertained and feasted" Massasoit, the Native Americans' "greatest king" and ninety of his tribe for three days, during which time their guests "went out and killed five deer." Winslow, reporting back to fellow Puritans in England, concluded that: "although it be not always so plentiful as it was at this time with us, yet by the goodness of God, we are so far from want that we often wish you partakers of our plenty."

THANKSGIVING

The traditional origins of Thanksgiving in the United States lie in the three-day feast that brought together the Plymouth colonists and the Wampanoag Indians in 1621. It was a celebration of survival: the Native Americans had helped the colony through the harsh winter of that year. In 1863, President Abraham Lincoln proclaimed Thanksgiving as a holiday, to be observed annually on the fourth Thursday in November.

Puritans traveled across the Atlantic with the aim of constructing a religious community in the New World. They encountered an America which seemed to be a bountiful place reserved for them through an act of divine benevolence. Indeed, even when their harvests failed, they ascribed it to their own religious back-sliding rather than an inhospitable environment. So when Roger Williams founded the capital of Rhode Island, it was appropriately named "Providence": God's gift to the faithful. The irony was, as the historian Daniel Boorstin pointed out, that the Puritans failed to keep their communities intact as they moved "from providence to pride." Over time, they began to take credit for their own achievements in establishing vibrant and self-sustaining colonies in America, rather than attributing their success to the progressive unfolding of God's plan.

Nevertheless, the influence of their religion was felt beyond the colonies initially established in New England. One of the leaders of the wave of religious revivalism that swept through the colonies – the "Great Awakening" of the mid-seventeenth century – was Jonathan Edwards, many of whose beliefs bear witness to the Puritan heritage in Massachusetts where his mission began. Edwards, together with other preachers such as George Whitfield, inspired congregations and communities across America to embrace religious activism rather than passively accept the authority of their ministers. The "Great Awakening" was an evangelical movement which led many to embrace individual religious freedom, even to the extent of rejecting the church as a formal conduit of faith. It inculcated a sense of rebellion among a generation of Americans swept up in its fervor, which later found political expression in the demand for political independence from Britain.

Moreover, the belief that the European discovery of America was part of the Creator's plan for the future of humanity continued to suffuse the rhetoric which encouraged the continental expansion of the United States during the nineteenth century.

In 1839, John L. O'Sullivan wrote an article in the *United States Democratic Review* in which he argued that "we may confidently assume that our country is destined to be the great nation of futurity." America, he proclaimed, had been chosen (by whom he did not say, but his readers would have had no doubt that a divine presence was responsible) "to establish on earth the moral dignity and salvation of man – the immutable truth and beneficence of God." Six years later he repeated a similar assertion and coined the phrase that was subsequently widely quoted in support of American expansionism. It was now the "Manifest Destiny" of the United States to acquire additional territories, by force if necessary (at the time, O'Sullivan was promoting the case for the annexation of Texas from Mexico), not least to provide land for its increasing immigrant population. America's task, therefore, was "to overspread the continent allotted by Providence for the free development of our yearly multiplying millions."

MANIFEST DESTINY

Manifest Destiny was a phrase coined by John O'Sullivan in the *Democratic Review* in 1845 in support of the nineteenth-century ambition to add to the territory of the United States as its population increased and moved westwards. It suggested that such expansion was inevitable as part of a providential mission that would project the values of republican democracy across the American continent.

As Jefferson's vision of an "empire for liberty" stretching from the Atlantic to the Pacific oceans began to be realized during the nineteenth century, it confirmed the widespread belief that this achievement represented the unfolding of the nation's providential Manifest Destiny. It was a mission that connected religious rhetoric and secular faith in republican democracy as an ideal form of government. When, in the early twentieth century, the United States became increasingly involved in world affairs, such ideas continued to influence attitudes and opinions. Woodrow Wilson – a President whose views were shaped by his staunch religious beliefs – argued for American involvement in the First World War in order to "keep the world safe for democracy." Wilson's justification for bringing the United States into the European conflict linked America's national security with its mission to promote its democratic values throughout the world. His successors in the White House, notably during the Cold War and at the start of the contemporary "war on terror," used a similar rhetoric in arguing the necessity for military action overseas.

New England Puritans demanded religious conformity. Dissenters were expelled: Roger Williams was exiled in 1636 and founded the colony of Rhode Island on the principle of religious tolerance. He established a Baptist church in Providence. Later in the seventeenth century, Jewish settlers, discriminated against in Europe and who had already found refuge in New York and other Atlantic coastal towns, arrived to live alongside Baptists in Newport. Quakers from Britain, some of whom who had moved to New Jersey to escape persecution, also migrated in increased numbers to Pennsylvania after it was founded in 1681 by William Penn. Rhode Island and Pennsylvania proved to be more tolerant of religious diversity than the Puritan settlements of New England. Other Protestant denominations from continental Europe, including many Lutherans from Germany, settled there. Catholics were not to be out-done. In 1632, George Calvert, a convert to the faith, persuaded Charles 1 to grant Maryland a royal charter as, he hoped, a place where the religion would flourish free from the prejudice that it evoked in contemporary Britain. Catholics, however, formed an ever smaller proportion of the colony's population and after 1689 became increasingly embattled as they were subject to British laws restricting their religious liberty and political rights.

By the time of the American Revolution, therefore, the colonies had become religiously diverse with new denominations arriving to take their place alongside established faiths. In 1784, for example, the Methodist Episcopal Church was established in Baltimore. In 1786, the year before the Philadelphia Convention met to discuss the United States Constitution, Virginia enacted its "Statute for Religious Freedom," which had been drafted by Thomas Jefferson in 1777, the year after he wrote the Declaration of Independence. Jefferson argued that religious beliefs should not play a part in shaping the social contract: "our civil rights have no dependence on our religious opinions any more than our opinions in physics or geometry." Virginia's statute thus established not only the principle of the separation of church and state that influenced the constitutional thought of James Madison, among others, but also respected freedom of religion, enshrined in the first amendment of the Bill of Rights.

The "Great Awakening" had encouraged many Americans – including black Americans – to reaffirm their faith by joining the Baptist church. Encouraged by expansionist missionary activity, Baptists became the most numerous among the different Protestant denominations in most southern states. By 1845, however, growing tensions over the issues of slavery led to a parting of the ways between northern and southern Baptists. The Southern Baptist Convention would in time grow into the largest Protestant community in the United States, and indeed the world. Although Jefferson argued for a more secular society, religion – notably in the South – continued to be of central significance in shaping the politics of the nation.

When Tocqueville toured America in the 1830s he recognized the importance of religion in sustaining what was then seen as America's experiment with republican democratic government. It established a moral compass for a country that was constantly arguing about its future direction. Moreover it was Christianity rather than Judaism, Islam or any other faith which provided this pivotal point of reference. In the United States, as Tocqueville observed, Christianity "reigns without obstacle, by universal consent; the consequence is … that every principle of the moral world is fixed and determinate, although the political world is abandoned to the debates and experiments of men." Moreover, as Tocqueville realized "while the law permits Americans to do what they please, religion prevents them from conceiving, and forbids them to commit, what is rash and unjust." His conclusion was that adherence to religious beliefs was "more needed in democratic republics than in any others." Unfettered liberty threatened to dissolve into social anarchy.

Authoritarian governments or those based upon class structures that gave power to monarchs or aristocrats could restrict individual freedoms. In a republic, however, the people were sovereign, and they were deferential only to their own authority. Religion offered a countervailing power to supplement the constitutional system of checks and balances, preserving Americans against the potential damage caused by an excess of individual liberty. Tocqueville saw the problem: "how is it possible that society should escape destruction if the moral tie is not strengthened in proportion as the political tie is relaxed? And what can be done with a people who are their own masters if they are not submissive to the Deity?" The answer to both questions was to acknowledge the role of religion in shaping political life in America's democratic republic. In 1836, the historian George Bancroft gave an Independence Day oration in Springfield, Massachusetts in which he argued that "the United States, eminently the land of democracy, is the most religious country on earth." Political arguments in the United States are frequently articulated in a language combining what Tocqueville called the "spirit of religion" and the "spirit of freedom" in American life. Indeed, as Daniel Boorstin observed, there is a "mingling of political and religious thought" that he regarded as a characteristic of the peculiar and particular "genius of American politics."

The great moral causes that have impacted upon American political life have been often framed in a religious context. Before the Civil War, religious reformers were prominent among the advocates of the abolition of slavery. At the end of the nineteenth century they supported temperance and encouraged Americans toward sobriety. In 1920, the eighteenth amendment to the Constitution banned the production, sale and transportation of alcohol, although its unintended consequences might have given pause to those who believe in legal solutions to moral problems. Prohibition gave license to organized crime to supply the nation's demand for what was now an illegal substance, and fortunes were made during the thirteen years before the amendment was repealed.

Darwin in America

Abraham Lincoln and Charles Darwin were born on the same day: February 12, 1809. Fifty years later, on November 24, 1859, Lincoln was pursuing his career as a lawyer in Illinois. A little under twelve months later than that he would be elected President of the United States. That same day, Charles Darwin published his work on the *Origin of Species*. His ideas of evolution and natural selection ignited a firestorm of controversy among those who based their faith on the biblical accounts of creationism, particularly in the United States, where the argument still rages. Darwin revolutionized scientific thought. At the same time, Lincoln rose to the biggest political challenge of the nineteenth century: preserving the union through the catharsis of Civil War. Born continents apart and in very different circumstances, Lincoln and Darwin remain among the most influential of those whose actions and ideas continue to shape American politics and society.

After the Civil War, the United States entered a period of unprecedented industrial expansion. Capitalist enterprise was the engine that now drove the American economy forward, creating vast fortunes for some that also served to emphasize the increasing inequalities in the distribution of the nation's wealth. Why did some gain and others lose? Darwin's work could provide an answer. Translating his ideas from natural science to social science, a new generation of sociologists – William Graham Sumner was prominent among them – argued that "Social Darwinism" implied a natural order in which the competition of the market economy encouraged "the survival of the fittest." "Social Darwinism" appealed to the generation of American business-men who made their fortunes after the Civil War. Indeed one of them, Andrew Carnegie, revealed in his autobiography how he had "found the truth of evolution."

In 1889, Carnegie, who had become one of America's most successful industrialists, and who was then able to pay himself an annual salary of $25 million, wrote an essay entitled "The Gospel of Wealth." While he believed – unsurprisingly – that there should be no constraints on the free-wheeling capitalist system which had allowed him to amass his fortune, he neverthe-less accepted that there should be an element of social responsibil-ity among the wealthy. They should, in effect, be trustees. Indeed, in his view "the accumulation of wealth should be followed by its distribution in the form of public endowments." Carnegie not only preached his "Gospel of Wealth," he also practiced it. He became one of the most generous philanthropists in American his-tory, contributing to a number of charitable causes, notably the establishment of public libraries and other educational institutions.

Carnegie's example was followed by others. John D. Rockefeller, whose wealth was based on his appreciation that oil would be essential to the smooth running of the new industrial economy, retired in 1897 and became a major benefactor of the University of Chicago. On his death in 1937, he had successfully disposed of most of his fortune. Carnegie, Rockefeller and others established a practice of private philanthropy that has influenced the conduct of the wealthy in America ever since. In this sense, Bill Gates, the founder of Microsoft, in establishing his charitable foundation in 1994, is heir to a tradition that will out-live his own contribution to it.

Philanthropy can be born of a religious conscience, or at least implies an appreciation of the biblical injunction that "it is hard for a rich man to enter the kingdom of heaven." Yet even if earthly fortunes are given away to benefit the community, the generosity of the rich cannot solve all the problems of a capitalist society.

There were many who did not make their fortunes in the post-Civil War era. Some who witnessed the poor social conditions and visible inequalities that characterized America's industrial economy of the late nineteenth century voiced their concerns by expressing their criticism in terms of their religious faith. The "Social Gospel" appealed to liberal and progressive Protestants who emphasized Christian values and tried to align them with political action to alleviate the problems of poverty, crime and social exclusion prevalent in the United States. Walter Rauschenbusch, a Baptist minister from New York, became a leading theologian in this movement. His parish included the infamous "Hell's Kitchen" area of Manhattan where social problems were at their most acute. From his experiences there, Rauschenbusch argued in *Christianity and the Social Crisis* (1907) that the society which allowed such conditions was the embodiment of sin. Moreover, it became society's obligation as much as an individual's responsibility to fight such evil in order to achieve a state of grace.

The "Social Gospel" imparted a religious rhetoric to the progressive movement of the late nineteenth and early twentieth centuries. Among those politicians who embraced its concerns was William Jennings Bryan, the liberal Democrat and devout Presbyterian who was nominated and who ran unsuccessfully for the presidency on three occasions. Yet at the end of his life,

Bryan also played an important role in the emergence of another religious movement which would in time become one of the most conservative forces in contemporary American politics: fundamentalism.

Fifty years after the *Origin of Species* was published, the preface to another book, *The Fundamentals: A Testimony to the Truth*, recounted how:

> God moved two Christian laymen to set aside a large sum of money for issuing twelve volumes that would set forth the fundamentals of the Christian faith, and which were to be sent free to ministers of the gospel, missionaries, Sunday School superintendents, and others engaged in aggressive Christian work throughout the English speaking world.

These volumes were the outcome of a theological disagreement. They took issue with a group known as "higher critics," who studied the literary structure of the Bible and who saw it as a book that was a reflection of the views of those who wrote it. Modern interpretations of the Bible should appreciate it as an historical text. The "fundamentalists" disagreed. They saw the Bible as the literal truth that should be treated as God's word.

Darwin's theories challenged orthodox religious beliefs and in particular the biblical account of creationism. It is no surprise, therefore, that fundamentalists should be among those most offended by the scientific theory of evolution. It was William Jennings Bryan's campaign against the teaching of Darwin's theory of evolution in American schools which forced fundamentalism from the fringes of theological debate into the center of the political spotlight. In 1925, the Bible was placed on trial in a courtroom in a small American town in Tennessee. Earlier that year the state had prohibited the teaching of evolution. In July, John Scopes, a Tennessee teacher, was prosecuted for violating that law and for telling his students, in the words of one of them, "all about monkeys and things."

The trial seized the national imagination. Scopes was found guilty and fined, although the verdict was subsequently overturned on appeal. The centerpiece of the proceedings was when Bryan, appearing as a witness for the prosecution, was cross-examined by Clarence Darrow, acting for the American Civil Liberties Union and one of the leading trial lawyers of the day. Darrow forced Bryan to concede that biblical stories were open to interpretation, exposing fundamentalist beliefs to public ridicule, not least from H.L. Mencken, who reported the trial. Bryan died five days after the verdict was given. His side had won the case but lost the argument in the court of public opinion. If he had lived, as Mencken observed, he "would be standing before the country today as a comic figure, tattered and preposterous." Fundamentalists retreated from the political arena only to re-emerge in the late twentieth century as a far better organized and more influential force in American society.

The church and Civil Rights

In March 2008, while campaigning for the Democrats' presidential nomination, Barack Obama was forced to deal with a firestorm of controversy that focused directly on the use of religious rhetoric. The incendiary statements of the Reverend Jeremiah Wright – the pastor of the United Church of Christ on Chicago's South Side, where Obama had been a longstanding member of the congregation – that black Americans should sing "God damn America" rather than "God Bless America" threatened to derail his campaign. In the speech he made in Philadelphia in March 2008 ("A More Perfect Union") in which he successfully defused the issue, Obama argued that Wright's language was the product of his involvement in the Civil Rights struggles of the 1950s and 1960s, in which black churches had played a key role. Like the white Protestant communities of the South and

Midwest, the political frustrations of the then disenfranchised black community found expression in the solidarity of their religion. Indeed, black churches had played a pivotal role within the Civil Rights movement.

Religion in the United States has been historically segregated not only by denominations of different faiths but also because of race. After the Civil War, the formal and informal networks of discrimination that existed across America meant that African-American churches remained separate places of worship reserved to the communities that attended them. In many ways, America today remains most divided when it is at prayer. The shocked reaction at the Reverend Wright's inflammatory sermons when they were replayed to a nationwide audience in part demonstrated the extent to which hitherto such rhetoric had remained unheard beyond the confines of the black church.

Moreover, Barack Obama's response to the controversy engendered by Wright's words to his congregation acknowledged the historical reality that shapes contemporary American religious life. In his speech in Philadelphia, Obama observed that:

> like other predominantly black churches across the country, Trinity embodies the black community in its entirety – the doctor and the welfare mom, the model student and the former gang-banger. Like other black churches, Trinity's services are full of raucous laughter and sometimes bawdy humor. They are full of dancing, clapping, screaming and shouting that may seem jarring to the untrained ear. The church contains in full the kindness and cruelty, the fierce intelligence and the shocking ignorance, the struggles and successes, the love and yes, the bitterness and bias that make up the black experience in America.

It was an insight into a form of worship that many among his white audience were unaware was taking place at the same time as they attended their own neighborhood churches.

During the 1950s and 1960s, for many black Americans, the church became a galvanizing force in advancing the cause of Civil Rights. The movement, with the Reverend Martin Luther King Jr. as its most prominent activist, was built around such organizations as the Southern Christian Leadership Conference. This was formed in the aftermath of the successful Montgomery Bus Boycott in Alabama (1955–1956). After Rosa Parks was arrested when she ignored the driver's order to give up her seat to a white man on a city bus, blacks protested by refusing to use public transportation while it remained segregated. King, who was himself arrested and jailed during the campaign for Civil Rights and who was awarded the Nobel Peace Prize, influenced Americans through his words as well as his actions. His most famous speech was given at the Lincoln Memorial during the 1963 "March on Washington." Its impact illustrates once more the influence of the language of religion in shaping American political rhetoric, not least in its famous peroration:

> Let freedom ring. And when this happens, and when we allow freedom to ring – when we let it ring from every village and every hamlet, from every state and every city, we will be able to speed up that day when all of God's children – black men and white men, Jews and Gentiles, Protestants and Catholics – will be able to join hands and sing in the words of the old Negro spiritual: "Free at last! Free at last! Thank God Almighty, we are free at last!"

On the other hand, radical black leaders saw King's religion as another manifestation of oppression. Malcolm X put it bluntly when he proclaimed that "Christianity is a white man's religion." Rejecting both King's faith and his non-violent approach to the achievement of Civil Rights, Malcolm X initially embraced the teachings of Elijah Muhammad and the Nation of Islam. In 1964, he broke with Muhammad and shortly before his assassination had become a Sunni Muslim, a religious path also followed by his most famous convert, the three times world heavy-weight boxing champion, Muhammad Ali. For some black Christians, the opposing views of King and Malcolm X produced a crisis of faith that was only resolved through the development of a new synthesis of religious beliefs. James Cone was prominent in exploring the ideas which formed the basis of black liberation theology. In Cone's words: "the burning theological question was, how can I reconcile Christianity and Black Power, Martin Luther King, Jr.'s idea of nonviolence, and Malcolm X's 'by any means necessary philosophy?'"

Cone argued that:

> the only option we blacks have is to fight in every way possible, so that we can create a definition of freedom based on our own history and culture. We must not expect white people to give us freedom. Freedom is not a gift, but a responsibility, and thus must be taken against the will of those who hold us in bondage.

Moreover, as Cone observed, according to Luke's gospel, Jesus had defined his mission on earth: "to proclaim release to the captives ... To set at liberty those who are oppressed" – in other words to act as a liberator. This interpretation of the Christian message thus placed its emphasis not only on its sympathy for the dispossessed – which Cone argued that the white church neglected – but also on the need for black churches to preach to their congregations that their faith should be one which empowers them in their struggle against the inherent racism of American society. This liberation theology allowed blacks to accommodate their religious beliefs to the contemporary political radicalism of the black power movement without following Malcolm X in rejecting Christianity in favor of Islam. It also meant that in black churches ministers like Jeremiah Wright would preach to congregations that understood them within the context of this radicalized faith.

Indeed, in a speech he made in 2006, the then Senator Barack Obama appreciated this radical role that black churches had assumed in American society. He drew attention to "the power of the African-American religious tradition to spur social change ... Because of its past, the black church understands in an intimate way the biblical call to feed the hungry and clothe the naked and challenge powers and principalities." Obama also acknowledged the influence of his Chicago church in his own religious development: "in its historical struggles for freedom and the rights of man, I was able to see faith as more than just a comfort to the weary or a hedge against death; it is an active, palpable agent in the world. It is a source of hope." Indeed it was from one of the Reverend Wright's sermons that Obama would take the title of his second book, *The Audacity of Hope*, which became in effect the manifesto for his presidential campaign. The black church and its liberation theology have continued to play a vital role in the promotion of Civil Rights and social justice in America. This activism of the left in many respects draws from the same well that had irrigated the Social Gospel in an earlier century. It coexists with the activism of the religious right, the socially conservative movement which has become increasingly vociferous as it tries to shape the moral landscape of contemporary American life.

The political influence of the religious right

Four assassinations – John F. Kennedy, Malcolm X, Martin Luther King Jr. and Robert Kennedy – punctuated American politics in the 1960s. In the following decade, the revelations of the Watergate scandal and the debacle that accompanied the end of the Vietnam

War further punctured the nation's confidence in its political system and its military capacity. One way out of the traumas afflicting contemporary America was to seek religion. In a Gallup poll in 1976, almost half of those Protestants questioned revealed that they had been "born again": wiping the slate clean, they had reaffirmed the centrality of faith in their lives. One of them was Jimmy Carter. In that same year, the former Governor of Georgia surfed the wave of popular revulsion against the political establishment in Washington DC (which had supplied the nation's Presidents for the previous two decades) first to the Democrats nomination and then to the White House.

Carter's religiosity was central to his campaign, not as a potential threat to his ambition to become President – as Kennedy's Catholicism had been in 1960 – but as a promise that encouraged the religiously committed to his side. He was among those described, not entirely inaccurately, by the journalist and novelist Tom Wolfe, as inspired by the "missionary lectern pounding Amen ten-finder C-major-chord Sister-Martha at the Yamaha-keyboard oblolly piney-woods Baptist faith in which the members of the congregation stand up and 'give witness' and 'share it, Brother' and 'share it, Sister' and 'praise God' during the service." Fellow evangelicals, whose political affiliations had previously been typically Republican, supported Carter, only to be disillusioned when, once in the White House, they found that he firmly rebuffed their agenda of religious regeneration. Although Carter was personally "pro-life" rather than "pro-choice" – a stance which gained him evangelical support – he remained true to his campaign promise not to undermine the Supreme Court's decision in *Roe v. Wade* by refusing to back a proposal for a constitutional amendment outlawing abortion. By 1980, therefore, evangelicals for whom this represented a betrayal of their faith were looking for a candidate who more faithfully represented their views on this "hot button" issue in American politics. In that year's presidential election, better organized and in greater numbers, they returned to the Republican fold and voted overwhelmingly for another self-proclaimed born again Christian, but one who thought *Roe v. Wade* should be overturned: Ronald Reagan.

As President, Reagan reached out to those whose political activism was informed by their strongly held religious views. Although he had made his career in Hollywood – which many evangelicals believed was a morally corrupting influence in American society – and despite the fact that he was divorced, Reagan seemed to be one of them. At least he talked the right language. On March 8, 1983, in a speech to the National Association of Evangelicals in Florida, in what Edmund Morris, his biographer, described as "a lay sermon from start to finish," Reagan defended his conviction that the inalienable rights set out in the Declaration of Independence were indeed God given. Such faith meant his administration was, the President suggested, "in opposition to, or at least out of step with, a prevailing attitude of many who have turned to a modern day secularism." On contemporary moral issues – among which abortion remained the most controversial – Reagan placed himself firmly on the side of the religious right. Moreover, given that communism was a self-proclaimed atheistic ideology, it could not lay claim to any moral high ground. Instead, in denying people their God given rights, Marxist-Leninist leaders had demonstrated the essential character of their revolution. The President asked his audience: "Let us pray for the salvation of all those who live in that totalitarian darkness ... the focus of evil in the modern world." Like him, they must recognize that they lived in a world dominated by "the struggle between right and wrong, good and evil."

Reagan's speech is a good example of how he used religious rhetoric to infuse political argument, particularly when addressing a particular and partisan audience of evangelist activists. The distinguished historian Henry Steele Commager called it "the worst presidential speech in American history" due to its "gross appeal to religious prejudice." Yet the criticism missed an important point. By the 1980s, the religious right had emerged as a force in American politics. Evangelical in its desire for fundamentalist change in an American society it regarded as secular, immoral and corrupt, it saw the Republican party as the vehicle for its ambition and, with the right occupant in the White House, it viewed the presidency as the "bully pulpit" from which its views might be proclaimed.

The influence of the religious right in contemporary American politics can be seen in terms of a process of constant reinvention. It has emerged from temporary setbacks to remain a constant presence in American political life. So in 1988, Pat Robertson, the southern Baptist minister whose success as a "televangelist" had helped make his Christian Broadcasting Network the largest of its kind in America, ran for the Republican presidential nomination. Despite an initial strong showing in the Iowa caucuses, where he came second behind Senator Bob Dole, beating the eventual nominee, Vice-President George Bush, into third place, his campaign failed to gain momentum and collapsed before the end of the primary season.

Electoral setbacks merely inspired Robertson into fresh organizational efforts. After his failure to win the Republican nomination in 1988, he put together a new "Christian Coalition" which waged a constant campaign on issues at the local level as well during state and national elections. Under the leadership of Ralph Read, who appeared on the cover of *Time* magazine in 1995 accompanied by the headline: "the right hand of God," coalition activists were perceived as the militant tendency in Republican grass roots politics, able in theory – if not always in practice – to deliver strong support to candidates who carried their endorsement. In 1992, at the Republican Convention in Houston, Robertson castigated Bill Clinton for "running on a platform that calls for saving the Spotted Owl, but never once mentions the name of God." President George Bush, anxious not

to alienate Robertson's supporters, endorsed the sentiment but
paid a political price. His failure to win re-election to the White
House was in part attributable to a widespread concern among
more moderate Republicans that the religious right had gained
too much influence within the party.

During the 1994 mid-term elections, when the Republicans
captured control of both Houses of Congress, the Christian
Coalition claimed some of the credit and lobbied for its own
"Contract with the American Family" as a supplement to the
party's "Contract with America." Among other issues, this manifesto argued for the allowance of "communal prayer in public
schools and courthouses," the abolition of the federal Department
of Education, "strict limits on abortion," controls on pornogra-
phy on cable television channels and the internet, together with
requirements for "prisoners to study and work" and to provide
"restitution to victims subsequent to prisoner's release." Moreover,
it was among the morally outraged and religiously fundamentalist members of the Republican party, particularly in the House of
Representatives, that the clamor was loudest in favor of bringing
impeachment proceedings against President Bill Clinton,
following the revelations of his liaison with a White House intern,
Monica Lewinsky.

Following the controversial presidential election of 2000,
George W. Bush took his place as the most overtly religious Chief
Executive since Jimmy Carter, and his re-election in 2004 was in
part due to, and met with the approval of, what was by now the
entrenched Christian fundamentalist wing of the Republican
party. Their continuing influence was shown in 2008, when the
former southern Baptist pastor Mick Huckabee, a believer in
the Bible as literal truth and who (like Bill Clinton) had been
governor of Arkansas, made a strong showing before being beaten
to the Republican nomination by John McCain.

In the mid-term elections of 2010, Christine O'Donnell
drew national attention and derision when she claimed that

evolution was a myth. If it was real, she asked, "why aren't monkeys still evolving into humans?" As a representative of the insurgent Tea Party movement, O'Donnell had captured the Republican nomination for the Senate seat in Delaware that had been vacated by Joe Biden when he became Vice-President. When she later appeared to argue that the Constitution draws no separation between church and state (despite the fact that the first amendment makes this explicit) political credulity was further strained. O'Donnell was defeated. The conviction politicians of the religious right can have difficulty appealing to a broader constituency than those who share their faith.

The medium and the message

It is not the catchiest of titles, but *The Whole Booke of Psalmes Faithfully Translated into English Metre* (1640) was the first book to be produced in America, by Stephen Daye, a printer in the Massachusetts Bay Colony. Also known as *The Bay Psalm Book*, along with the Bible (which had either accompanied the settlers across the Atlantic or was easily imported to the New World until trade was embargoed during the War of Independence), it became one of the most widely owned books in the New England colonies. It was later joined on Puritan bookshelves by *The New England Primer*, a self-help children's guide that explained the religious values of the communities into which they had been born. Various editions of the primer were published, selling an estimated five million copies between 1683 and 1830. Cheap to buy and highly portable, these were the fundamental texts of Puritanism. In 1663, John Eliot, one of the editors of the *Bay Psalm Book*, produced the first Bible printed in America. The outcome of his missionary work among the Native Americans, Eliot achieved the remarkable feat of translating the Gospel into Algonquin, a language that hitherto had remained unwritten.

These Puritan texts and Eliot's Bible are early examples of the role of the media – in this case the printing press – in spreading God's word to the faithful and among those whom they labored to convert.

As new media technologies have been invented and developed, religious denominations in the United States have been quick to press them into the service of their faith. In the twentieth century, first radio and then television allowed preachers to reach nationwide audiences and to gain political influence. During the 1930s, for example, Father Charles Coughlin, a Catholic priest, had an audience of over forty million listeners each week and was broadcasting on his own radio network from his church in Detroit. Coughlin was an early supporter of Franklin Roosevelt and the New Deal but by the end of the decade his rhetoric was much changed. His sermons, increasingly antisemitic and xenophobic, became virulent attacks on the President as Coughlin's political views hardened into support for Europe's fascist dictators. The "Radio Priest" remained a political force until he was effectively silenced after the Roosevelt administration introduced regulations that restricted and then denied his access to the airwaves.

If Coughlin had demonstrated the potential power of radio to preach to a national audience, the invention of television allowed equally charismatic preachers to enter their congregations' homes and to build their "electronic churches" as wealthy and successful enterprises. Among the pioneering "televangelists" was Oral Roberts, who began broadcasting his "healing tent" revival meetings, where he preached to audiences of thousands. In 1968 he enlisted Hollywood expertise to introduce his "electronic church," featuring celebrity guests in prime-time specials which attracted millions of followers across America. In addition to Pat Robertson, who used his church to launch his political career, other prominent "televangelists" included Jerry Falwell, Jimmy Swaggart and Jim Bakker. Personal and financial scandals eventually undermined their ministries, which, if they survived, continued to seek an audience of the faithful on cable and satellite networks.

Where the "electronic church" sought political influence it was in association with the Christian Right. Reversing his view that religious leaders should stay aloof from politics, in 1979 Jerry Falwell founded the "Moral Majority." At its peak it became one of the largest conservative lobby groups in the United States. A decade after it was established, lack of donations had eroded its financial base to the point where Falwell decided to wind up the organization, claiming it had fulfilled its purpose. Others followed his lead and filled the political vacuum that he had left. Pat Robertson's Christian Coalition network took over some of the remnants of Falwell's organization. "Focus on the Family," founded by James Dobson and based in Colorado Springs, also assumed a prominent role as an evangelical pressure group. In the 2008 presidential election, its preferred Republican candidate was Mick Huckabee and it only declared its support for the nominee, John McCain, after he selected Sarah Palin as his running mate. Dobson described Palin as "a solid conservative who has a reputation for espousing common sense." Her presence on the Republican ticket was, he suggested, "a very encouraging sign" for McCain's campaign, which had hitherto struggled to appeal to the Christian conservative wing of the party.

The "city upon a hill"

In his Farewell Address to the nation in 1989, Ronald Reagan confessed that as he was preparing to leave the White House he had from time to time been thinking "of the 'shining city upon a hill'." He went on to explain that "the phrase comes from John Winthrop, who wrote it to describe the America he imagined." Reagan identified with Winthrop: "an early Pilgrim, an early freedom man," even though as a former actor he was ad-libbing from the Puritan sermon Winthrop had made on the *Arbella*, sailing to America in 1630. Winthrop had described how the New England colony should think of itself: "we must consider that we shall be as a city upon a hill." It was a reference to America as the new Jerusalem: an image that could still stir the imagination of a President almost four hundred years later. Winthrop also told his fellow travelers that "the eyes of all people are upon us." If successful, the Puritan's community would be an example to the rest of the world.

Those, like Winthrop, who came to America in search of religious freedom have since exercised a powerful hold on the nation's imagination. Despite Reagan's admiration, however, at times, Puritan insistence on religious conformity has been used to illustrate the potential excesses of political intolerance. For example, in 1953, at the height of the anti-communist hysteria provoked by the investigations and increasingly wild allegations of Senator Joseph McCarthy, in *The Crucible*, the playwright Arthur Miller dramatized the Salem witch-hunt trials that had taken place at the end of the seventeenth century in Puritan New England. American audiences could easily make the allegorical connection between the present and the past. More recently, Kenneth Starr, the independent counsel whose investigations into alleged corruption in the Clinton White House set the scene for the President's impeachment, was widely portrayed in the media as a modern day Puritan witch-hunter.

Appreciating the significance of the nation's religious heritage is important in understanding contemporary American political culture. Religious references and invocations of faith – "God Bless America" – are part of everyday political discourse. Membership of a particular church can suggest a particular political persuasion. Some churches are broad, incorporating wide varieties of faith. Within American Protestantism, for example, evangelicals remain the most numerous grouping alongside other denominations, including the black church. Sometimes they may find common ground, but often their political attitudes are opposed. Fundamentalists in particular have provoked repeated skirmishes in America's "culture wars" over issues such as abortion, gay and women's rights, euthanasia and potential medical advances in stem cell research. Foreign policy attitudes – notably toward the Middle East and support for Israel – have been influenced not only by Christian interpretations of biblical prophecy but also by the well-financed, well-organized and well-connected Jewish lobby.

In 1812, the American Board of Commissioners for Foreign Missions was established during the religious revival of the pre-Civil War period known as the "Second Great Awakening." It supported Protestant activity to spread the Christian message overseas, not least in Hawaii, where in 1820, Hiram Bingham led the first group of American missionaries to the islands. In 1842 a school for the children of missionaries – later officially named as Oahu College – was opened on land originally given to Bingham and his wife. Its first teacher and president was the Reverend Daniel Dole. Throughout the nineteenth century, American missionaries not only continued to convert islanders to their faith, they were also an influence, directly or indirectly, in Hawaii's political life. Sanford Dole, who was born at his father's school in 1844, later participated in the revolution that overthrew the island's monarchy in 1893. He became president of the republic of Hawaii and after its annexation to the United States in 1900 he was its first territorial governor.

Oahu College was re-named Punahou School in 1934. In 1971, it became associated with another future President, this time of the United States, when the ten-year-old son of a Kenyan father and an American mother enrolled there. Barack Obama's school in Hawaii could by then claim to be one of the oldest independent schools in America, but in keeping with its origins, part of its mission remained to "develop moral and spiritual values consistent with the Christian principles on which Punahou was founded, affirming the worth and dignity of each individual." An enduring echo of the same religious ideals that had brought the first Puritans across the Atlantic to New England can be heard in the Pacific islands of Hawaii: the last state to join America's federal republic.

6

Foreign affairs and the idea of America abroad

American foreign policy is global in both its reach and its ambition. In terms of its military resources, it has no serious competitors. Its industrial, trading and financial engines continue to propel the world economy either into growth or, as was the case in 2008, into recession. The United States defines international tastes in pop and high culture. This combination of "hard power" (the capacity to exercise military force) and "soft power" (the influence of its example) makes America the dominant actor in world affairs. Yet the September 11, 2001 terrorist attacks on the World Trade Center in New York and the Pentagon in Washington DC demonstrated its vulnerability. America's response was to defend its democratic values in fighting two wars, in Afghanistan and in Iraq. Both proved to be difficult and costly campaigns. A foreign policy that seeks to project the "idea of America" abroad is open to both domestic and international criticism when it relies too heavily on seeking military solutions to political problems.

Since the early years of the republic, American foreign policy has been grounded in an acute awareness of potential threats to the new nation's survival. The War of Independence did not secure its borders. British troops remained on American soil. France and Spain retained an interest in North America. The United States faced a difficult task in navigating the often turbulent waters of contemporary European imperial rivalries. Presidential leadership was critical and it was George Washington who initially set the compass of American foreign policy. For the next hundred years, his successors in the White House influenced its direction as the United States developed its capacity to act on the world stage. Then in the twentieth century, which Henry Luce, the publisher of *Time* magazine, famously called "the American Century," the United States became the dominant force in international relations. At the same time, America's sense that it faces enduring threats to its national security continued to shape its foreign policy, during the Cold War and more recently in its conduct of the contemporary "war on terror." The fears which have shaped the nation's perspectives on the wider world are a critical influence in determining the way in which the United States acts and reacts when faced with the challenges of international relations.

THE AMERICAN CENTURY

In 1941, Henry Luce, the publisher of *Time* and *Life* magazines, encouraged his readers to "create the first great American Century." He urged the United States to enter the Second World War to promote democratic freedoms threatened by fascism. Luce argued that America should "exert upon the world the full impact of our influence, for such purposes as we see fit and by such means as we see fit." The United States should assume a dominant role in international relations rather than remain isolated from world affairs.

Isolationism and internationalism

Isolationism springs from a sense of self-containment. Protected by the oceans – the Atlantic and the Pacific – with its abundance of natural resources and land, its advocates argue that America does not need to become involved in world affairs. During the nineteenth century, moreover, remaining largely remote from elsewhere allowed the United States to focus on organizing itself as an independent nation. It was fully occupied in establishing and expanding its territorial control of the continent. Through the Louisiana Purchase (1803), the annexation of Texas (1845) and the war with Mexico (1846–1848), America pursued its Manifest Destiny westwards, although the political controversy surrounding the question as to whether slaves should be permitted to accompany the pioneers who occupied the new land ultimately threatened the future of the nation itself.

By the end of the nineteenth century, with the United States acknowledged as the dominant nation on the North American continent, the isolationist sentiment that had helped drive domestic expansionism was temporarily submerged by the wave of national approval for international engagement. One outcome of the Spanish-American War (1898) was an enduring American presence in Cuba and its military base at Guantanamo Bay. Victory also brought colonial possessions. The Philippines, Puerto Rico and Guam became part of an American empire in the Pacific. During the war, in a separate development, Hawaii, with its military base at Pearl Harbor, was also annexed.

Such a dramatic entrance on the world stage boosted national self-confidence but did not drown entirely the isolationist impulse. It revived within two decades when its supporters argued that the national interest might be best served by remaining aloof from the clashes in Europe that precipitated the First World War. Woodrow Wilson's success in overcoming opposition to America's eventual involvement in the European conflict was mirrored by his subsequent failure to persuade the Senate to ratify the Versailles Treaty. In December 1918, when Wilson crossed the Atlantic on the USS *George Washington* to take part in the peace negotiations at Versailles, he was at the height of his popularity as an international statesman. However, in the United States, his Republican opponents had already regained control of Congress in the mid-term elections of that year. The President returned home to a country once more persuaded that it should leave the rest of the world to its own devices.

The 1920s and 1930s marked the high water mark of twentieth-century isolationism as a powerful political force that did much to delay American entry into the Second World War, until the attack on Pearl Harbor provoked an inevitable response. After the war, with an unrivaled military potential and possessing nuclear weapons, the United States became, quite simply, the most powerful nation in the world. In itself this did much to undermine the argument for isolationism. If America was the most important actor in world affairs then it followed that it should at least try to play its part rather than remain back-stage. Internationalists argued that active engagement in world affairs was in the nation's self-interest. Moreover, they were convinced of the benefits of encouraging the spread of democratic republican values: the principles of liberty, equality and respect for human and civil rights. Their argument was simple and compelling: the "idea of America" abroad helped preserve national security at home. Internationalism colonized the moral high ground in its conviction that the necessity of American leadership is based on the assumption that the nation is a pre-eminent force for good in international affairs. Such idealism is an important principle in providing Americans with a justification for taking action in the international arena, not least when the nation has intervened militarily overseas. However, even though the United States did not retreat from engagement with the world in 1945 as it had in 1918, isolationist sentiment was a critical chorus throughout the Cold War. Its voice continues to be heard in contemporary debates over the direction of American foreign policy.

In 1790 Thomas Jefferson gave his opinion that "the transaction of business with foreign nations is Executive altogether." The

President has the responsibility for conducting the nation's foreign policy. It follows that, at critical junctures in the nation's history, Presidents have decided upon courses of action that have become touchstones for their successors when faced with similar problems. There is, indeed, a marked continuity in American foreign policy. The style may change but the substance remains the same: the nation's security in the face of perceived or actual threats from abroad is its paramount concern. In 1796, Washington's Farewell Address contained advice to his fellow Americans as to how the nation should conduct its foreign policy. Three years earlier, he had avoided taking sides in the war which had erupted between France and Britain, proclaiming instead that America would remain neutral in the conflict. Now he suggested that this would remain the best course of action in the future: "nothing is more essential than that permanent, inveterate antipathies against particular nations and passionate attachments for others should be excluded and that in place of them just and amicable feelings towards all should be cultivated." He confirmed that what he had in mind was the conduct of America toward contemporary Europe, that had "a set of primary interests which to us have none or a very remote relation." Washington remained convinced that "our detached and distant situation invites and enables us to pursue a different course." America should leave Europe to its own devices. The President posed the question: "why, by interweaving our destiny with that of any part of Europe, entangle our peace and prosperity in the toils of European ambition, rivalship, interest, humor or caprice?" It followed, therefore, that "it is our true policy to steer clear of permanent alliances with any portion of the foreign world."

Washington's argument appeared to present the case for isolationism. Yet he also recognized that there would be occasions when the United States had to engage with other nations in order to deal with potential threats to its future, "taking care always to keep ourselves by suitable establishments on a respectable defensive posture, we may safely trust to temporary alliances for extraordinary emergencies." The sentiments expressed in the Farewell Address demonstrated an awareness of the challenges facing the recently established republic. It represented a declaration of American independence in foreign affairs, aiming to give the new nation some freedom for maneuver in its diplomatic relations with other powers.

If Washington suggested the broad principles upon which America should base its international relations, it was left to his successors to define the terms of the nation's engagement with the wider world. In the nineteenth century, President Monroe gave his name to the doctrine that became a foundation stone of foreign policy. In the twentieth century, Theodore Roosevelt, Woodrow Wilson, Franklin Roosevelt and Harry Truman were the presidential architects of America's rise to international pre-eminence. The capacity of the Executive to map the contours of American foreign policy remains profound, but Presidents act with a clear sense of the directions set by their predecessors in the office.

The Monroe Doctrine and its corollaries

The relationship between the United States and its neighbors to the south has been historically often complex and sometimes fraught. This is in no small measure a legacy of European colonialism in both North and South America. In 1815, besides the US, there was only one other independent nation in the Americas: Haiti. By 1822, however, Spain's colonies on the South American mainland had either become independent republics or were fighting to free themselves from colonial control. Speculation mounted that the European powers were putting together a coalition of the willing to re-impose Spanish control over its former possessions even though the possibility remained more rumor than fact. Nevertheless it gave President Monroe the opportunity to use his annual message to Congress in December 1823 to issue a warning.

After observing that the United States had no interest in taking sides in the squabbles between European powers, Monroe drew a clear distinction between the republican forms of government which had been established across the Atlantic and the monarchies that still dominated the European political stage. "The political system of the allied powers is essentially different in this respect from that of America." There should be no attempt to re-introduce the form of government which had been decisively rejected by the former colonies into the new world. "We owe it, therefore, to candor and to the amicable relations existing between the United States and those powers to declare that we should consider any attempt on their part to extend their system to any portion of this hemisphere as dangerous to our peace and safety." Monroe established the principle that the United States had a sphere of influence over both the North and South American continents and that Europe should no longer assume that it could maintain or extend its colonial influence there.

For Europeans it remained an empty threat. The United States did not yet have the military capacity to give any real meaning to Monroe's words. For Americans, however, the President had made a significant statement of foreign policy. Two decades later it was already on the way to achieving the status of becoming the first – and best known – presidential doctrine. By then, however, what might have first appeared to be a message of support for independent republics established throughout the Americas was being re-cast as a statement which gave the United States a right to expand its borders in its own backyard. In his first annual message to Congress in December 1845, President James Polk, following the annexation of Texas, and with his eyes on the prize of California, reiterated Monroe's argument that European power politics should not be played out across the Atlantic. What he referred to as the "balance of power" maintained in Europe between its monarchies should not be extended across to republican America.

> We must ever maintain the principle that the people of this continent alone have the right to decide their own destiny. Should any portion of them, constituting an independent state, propose to unite themselves with our Confederacy, this will be a question for them and us to determine without any foreign interposition.

Texas would join the union at the end of the month in which Polk delivered his message.

The President also proclaimed it:

> a proper occasion to reiterate and reaffirm the principle avowed by Mr. Monroe and to state my cordial concurrence in its wisdom and sound policy … it should be distinctly announced to the world as our settled policy that no future European colony or dominion shall with our consent be planted or established on any part of the North American continent.

Polk's corollaries, which extended the provisions of the policy adopted by Monroe, claimed for the United States freedom of action in expanding its borders. California would become part of America after the war with Mexico, its immediate neighbor to the south.

Isolationism appeared as a two-way street: disengagement from the world had its counterpart in the demand for non-interference, in particular from Europe, in the quest for more territory in fulfillment of the United States' Manifest Destiny. For much of the nineteenth century, the Monroe Doctrine was largely inoperative outside America's immediate sphere of influence. The United States did not protest when Britain took over the Falkland Islands in 1833 and did not object to its efforts during the 1850s to extend its influence in Central America. In 1861, Spain was permitted to briefly regain control of its former colony of Santo Domingo before in 1865 it became the capital of the newly independent Dominican Republic.

In 1895, Richard Olney, President Grover Cleveland's Secretary of State, offered another corollary to the Monroe Doctrine in asserting the right of the United States to arbitrate a border dispute between British Guiana and Venezuela. He argued that:

> Today the United States is practically sovereign on this continent and its fiat is law upon the subjects to which it confines its interposition … its infinite resources combined with its isolated position render it master of the situation and practically invulnerable as against any or all other powers.

America now assumed the right to intervene in the affairs of other countries within its sphere of influence by virtue of its power and proximity to them.

Theodore Roosevelt went even further than this in 1904 when he proclaimed what became the most famous corollary to Monroe's Doctrine. Responding to contemporary European military threats toward nations such as Venezuela and the Dominican Republic, he re-asserted the claim that external powers should not involve themselves in the affairs of the Americas. At the same time, however, the United States now assumed the right to intervene in the internal politics of its neighbors to the south if it thought such action necessary. "If a nation shows that it knows how to act with reasonable efficiency and decency in social and political matters, if it keeps order and pays its obligations, it need fear no interference from the United States." However:

> chronic wrongdoing, or an impotence which results in a general loosening of the ties of civilized society, may in America, as elsewhere, ultimately require intervention by some civilized nation, and in the Western Hemisphere the adherence of the United States to the Monroe Doctrine may force the United States, however reluctantly, in flagrant cases of such wrongdoing or impotence, to the exercise of an international police power.

By the beginning of the twentieth century, the United States was in a position to make good on its pledge. Interventions followed in several South American and Caribbean countries. The "Colossus of the North" had parlayed the Monroe Doctrine into a foreign policy that extended its political influence throughout the Americas.

Progressive internationalism: Theodore Roosevelt and Woodrow Wilson

Theodore Roosevelt and Woodrow Wilson were the first two American Presidents to receive the Nobel Peace Prize: Roosevelt for his role in ending the Russian-Japanese War of 1905 and Wilson for acting as the architect of the League of Nations, even though his nation refused to enter the building. Roosevelt's award recognized a new international reality. At the beginning of the twentieth century, the White House was home to potential world leaders. The United States had become a powerful nation and its President could make critical interventions on the global stage. This much was confirmed in 1917 when Wilson asked Congress to declare war on Germany. It was only the fourth occasion that a President had made such a request as well as being the first time that the United States would enter a conflict in concert with other nations. If isolationists could tolerate such action as an example of Washington's "temporary alliances for extraordinary emergencies," they would reject Wilson's attempt to involve the United States in a more permanent organization designed to keep the peace. Nevertheless, the progressive internationalism embraced by Roosevelt and Wilson has become the most important influence in shaping the contemporary contours of American foreign policy.

Roosevelt's famous aphorism, "speak softly and carry a big stick," signaled his robust approach to promoting American interests in the wider world. The "big stick" was the American military – the navy and troops were deployed, for example, in support of the President's ambition to construct a canal across the Central American isthmus that would allow easy passage between the Pacific and Atlantic oceans. Roosevelt, in his announcement to Congress of the acquisition of the Panama Canal zone, was in no doubt that "the control, in the interest of the commerce and traffic of the whole civilized world, of the means of undisturbed transit across the Isthmus of Panama has become of transcendent importance to the United States." Building it took a decade, but when the canal opened in 1914 it had an immediate impact on the volume and flow of world trade. The strategic importance of the Panama Canal was self-evident. It confirmed America's status as an emerging world power. During the Spanish–American War in 1898, the USS *Oregon* was sent from San Francisco to the Caribbean. The voyage around Cape Horn took over two months. The short-cut across Panama enabled the American navy to move rapidly between the two oceans. Moreover, it was a navy second only to Britain's in terms of its size. Its global reach was symbolized in 1907, when Roosevelt had the ships painted white and sent the fleet on a goodwill tour around the world.

If Roosevelt's approach to foreign policy recognized America's capacity to influence the conduct of international relations, it was not at the expense of a strong isolationist sentiment within the United States which still advocated non-involvement in world affairs. When the First World War broke out in Europe, America's national interest seemed best served by taking its traditional stance of neutrality. When Woodrow Wilson argued the case for the United States to go to war in 1917, it thus represented a turning point in American foreign policy. Wilson had won re-election in 1916 with the slogan "he kept us out of war." Early in 1917, however, German submarines resumed indiscriminate attacks on shipping in the Atlantic, causing Wilson to sever diplomatic relations. His policy of "armed neutrality" was in tatters. Moreover, evidence from the "Zimmermann Telegram" suggested that Germany might ally itself with Mexico to go to war against the United States. On April 2, the President went to Congress to present the case for American military intervention in the European conflict.

It was Wilson who put forward the internationalist argument for America's active engagement with the world that has

ZIMMERMANN TELEGRAM

In January 1917 the British decoded a telegram from Arthur Zimmermann, the German foreign minister, sent to his country's ambassador to Mexico. It suggested that Germany would support Mexico's claims to regain territory lost to the United States in the nineteenth century if it declared war on America. Woodrow Wilson was informed of the contents of the telegram in February and details of it were reported in the American press early in March. News of Zimmermann's proposal inflamed anti-German sentiment in the United States and set the stage for the President's speech to Congress asking for a declaration of war.

resonated ever since in American foreign policy debates. Going beyond the simple assertion that German provocation was sufficient cause to take action, he also argued that going to war would advance the "idea of America" abroad and the ideals of American democracy. The President was convinced that:

> We are glad to fight thus for the ultimate peace of the world and for the liberation of its peoples ... for the rights of nations great and small ... The world must be made safe for democracy. Its peace must be planted upon the tested foundations of political liberty. We have no selfish ends to serve. We desire no conquest, no dominion ... We are but one of the champions of the rights of mankind. We shall be satisfied when those rights have been made as secure as the faith and the freedom of nations can make them.

Wilson took a long-term view. America's national security would be preserved by promoting democracy abroad as a way to build a lasting peace. The United States should go to war to make the world "safe for democracy": a war aim that suggests America has to defend not simply its geographical borders but also its republican values.

Since 1945, from Harry Truman to Barack Obama, Presidents have drawn from the well of Wilson's rhetoric to justify American military interventionism overseas. Yet America's principal overseas military interventions during this time – in Korea, Vietnam, Afghanistan and Iraq – have had limited success in advancing its democratic values, and domestic public opinion in the United States has questioned the link between military intervention and democracy promotion. Nevertheless, Woodrow Wilson, like Theodore Roosevelt, saw that presidential leadership was critical at a time when the United States was realizing its potential to act upon the world stage. He once wrote that "the President is at liberty both in law and conscience to be as big as he can." That was also the view of Roosevelt's cousin Franklin, the assistant secretary of the navy in Wilson's administration, who as President made critical contributions to the contours and the conduct of American foreign policy.

Franklin Roosevelt and foreign policy

Franklin Roosevelt entered the White House on March 4, 1933, a little over a month after Adolf Hitler was appointed Chancellor of Germany. Initially, however, the American President's pre-occupations were domestic. Picking up the pieces after the Wall Street Crash was his primary concern. As he observed in his first inaugural address, therefore:

> our international trade relations, though vastly important, are in point of time and necessity secondary to the establishment of a sound national economy. I favor as a practical policy the putting of first things first. I shall spare no effort to restore world trade by international economic readjustment, but the emergency at home cannot wait on that accomplishment.

He also outlined his foreign policy with respect to the countries to America's south. The United Sates would be, in his character-istically homely metaphor, a "good neighbor … who resolutely respects himself and, because he does so, respects the rights of others – the neighbor who respects his obligations and respects the sanctity of his agreements in and with a world of neighbors." In keeping with the prevailing isolationist mood in the nation, the foreign policy of the United States did not seek active engage-ment with the wider world if events did not impact directly on its domestic and continental concerns.

During the 1930s, the international impact of the economic depression led to the rise of fascism in Europe, and by the end of the decade Hitler had become anything but a good neighbor. Roosevelt could not ignore political developments across the Atlantic but enduring isolationist sentiment limited his capacity to pursue a more activist foreign policy that might have helped to delay or forestall what became an increasingly inevitable conflict. Between 1935 and 1939, Congress passed four neutrality acts designed to keep increasingly fractious world politics at arm's length. On September 3, 1939, two days after the Second World War broke out, in a "fireside chat" to the nation, Roosevelt pointed out the potential consequences of this continued policy of isolationism during wartime. "You must master at the outset a simple but unalterable fact in modern foreign relations between nations. When peace has been broken anywhere, the peace of all countries everywhere is in danger." He admitted that:

> it is easy for you and for me to shrug our shoulders and to say that conflicts taking place thousands of miles from the continental United States, and, indeed, thousands of miles from the whole American Hemisphere, do not seriously affect the Americas – and that all the United States has to do is to ignore them.

Yet, "passionately though we may desire detachment, we are forced to realize that … every ship that sails the sea, every battle that is fought does affect the American future." The President reassured his audience that "we seek to keep war from our own firesides by keeping war from coming to the Americas. For that we have historic precedent that goes back to the days of the administration of President George Washington." He would therefore accept that America's initial response to the international crisis should be to maintain a policy of neutrality even though "I cannot ask that every American remain neutral in thought as well." Certainly its Commander-in-Chief had no doubts where the nation's sympathies should lie, and during the next two years he did what he could, notably through "lend-lease" arrangements, to aid the allied war effort.

Even before Japan's attack on Pearl Harbor brought the United States into the conflict, Roosevelt had looked forward to peace. In August 1941, following his discussions with Winston Churchill, the United States and Britain had issued the Atlantic Charter. It outlined a post-war settlement that would include an end to imperialist expansionism, international economic cooperation and a "permanent system of general security" based on disarmament. On January 1, 1942, twenty-four other countries signed up to the Charter's provisions in a statement entitled, at Roosevelt's suggestion, a "Declaration by the United Nations." During the wartime conferences between Roosevelt, Churchill and Stalin, the outlines of the organization were agreed. It would have a security council with permanent membership for the war-time allies – America, Russia, Britain, France and China – and a general assembly with representatives from member nations.

If the United Nations was the forum in which nations might learn, in the words of Roosevelt's cousin, to "speak softly" with one another, the United States would end the Second World War by using the biggest stick that allied scientists and engineers could invent: the atomic bomb. In August 1939, the month before war broke out, Albert Einstein, who had escaped from Nazi anti-semitism to come to Princeton University, had written to the President warning him that the potential now existed for nuclear physics to produce such weapons. Roosevelt had authorized a secret program of research and development – the Manhattan Project – to ensure that the United States took the lead in such a development. He died in April 1945, just over three weeks before Hitler committed suicide in his Berlin bunker and three months before the successful test of a plutonium bomb in the New Mexican desert.

Roosevelt's impact on the direction of American foreign policy was profound. His legacy was to ensure that internationalism finally supplanted isolationism as the dominant theme in the formulation of American foreign policy, that the United Nations, with its headquarters in New York, existed, however imperfectly, as a forum for the preservation of world peace and that, as the first nuclear power, America emerged from the Second World War as the principal actor in world affairs.

Containment and the Truman Doctrine

In his campaign for an unprecedented fourth term in the White House, Roosevelt had changed his running mate from Henry Wallace to Harry Truman. So it was President Truman who, after Roosevelt's death, took the decision to drop atomic bombs on Japan. He was also the architect of America's Cold War foreign policy and the second Chief Executive to give his name to a doctrine. Japan surrendered on September 2, 1945. Within six months, post-war antagonisms between former allies had developed. In February 1946 George Kennan, then a diplomat in America's embassy in Moscow, sent a telegram (subsequently published as "The Sources of Soviet Conduct") from there to Washington, in which he argued that communism was an expansionist ideology and that the American response should be a policy of containment. In March, in a speech at Fulton in Truman's home state of Missouri, Churchill famously described what had happened in Europe: "from Stettin in the Baltic to Trieste in the Adriatic an iron curtain has descended across the Continent." Behind it formerly independent nations were "subject in one form or another, not only to Soviet influence but to a very high and, in some cases, increasing measure of control from Moscow." During 1947, Greece and Turkey seemed likely to join them. In requesting Congress to supply them with

economic and military aid, Truman formulated the doctrine to
which he gave his name.

The President argued that there were two options. "At the
present moment in world history nearly every nation must
choose between alternative ways of life." For Truman, "one way
of life is based upon the will of the majority, and is distinguished
by free institutions, representative government, free elections,
guarantees of individual liberty, freedom of speech and religion,
and freedom from political oppression." It was a reiteration of the
essential elements of the "idea of America" as a democratic
republic. Truman went on to describe its opposite, a totalitarian
regime "based upon the will of a minority forcibly imposed upon
the majority. It relies upon terror and oppression, a controlled
press and radio; fixed elections, and the suppression of personal
freedoms." The contrast between these two systems made his
conclusion self-evident: "I believe that it must be the policy of
the United States to support free peoples who are resisting
attempted subjugation by armed minorities or by outside pressures. I believe that we must assist free peoples to work out their
own destinies in their own way."

Later the same year, the National Security Council (NSC)
was set up within the White House to support the President in
the formulation of a foreign policy that was increasingly associated with the use of military force in the face of perceived threats
to national security. By 1949, the Soviet Union had developed an
atomic bomb. The potential for nuclear confrontation – dramatically demonstrated during the Cuban Missile Crisis in 1962 –
became and remained the concern of every American
Commander-in-Chief. Foreign and defense policy were thus
increasingly coordinated through the NSC as the forum that
brought together the President's national security adviser and the
Secretaries of State and Defense. Indeed, in 1950 a National
Security Council Report (NSC 68) recommended that the
United States develop "a level of military readiness which can be

maintained as long as necessary as a deterrent to Soviet aggression." The Cold War became a series of presidential judgment calls as to when and where to commit American forces in "limited wars" to deal with the perceived communist threat, principally in South America, Southeast Asia and the Caribbean.

Like Monroe, therefore, Truman gave his name to a doctrine which contrasted two systems of government and divided the world into two spheres of influence, one of which was on America's side and the other to which it should remain implacably opposed. Whereas Monroe's concerns were continental, however, Truman's were global. Containment and the Truman Doctrine committed the United States to resist communist expansion worldwide and, finally rejecting George Washington's advice, to help set up international networks of alliances – in 1949 the North Atlantic Treaty Organization (NATO) and in 1954 the Southeast Asia Treaty Organization (SEATO). Documents such as NSC 68 introduced a military dimension to both these cornerstones of Cold War foreign policy, persuading Truman of the necessity of taking action in Korea. A decade after the conclusion of the Korean War, it fell to President Lyndon Johnson to make a decision to commit the United States to another overseas military intervention to defend democracy and contain communism. America's war in Vietnam became its biggest military failure of the twentieth century, with repercussions that continue to impact on its foreign policy.

Defeat at the battle of Dien Bien Phu in 1954 ended France's attempt to re-impose the colonial control in Vietnam that it had lost during the Second World War. The country remained a Cold War battleground but President Eisenhower decided against direct American military intervention (the United States had provided material support for French forces there) so soon after the Korean war had been fought to an inconclusive stalemate. Instead, like Korea, Vietnam was divided in two: north and south.

Ho Chi Minh led the communist forces controlling the north. At the time of the Versailles conference, he had tried to meet with Woodrow Wilson to argue the case for Vietnamese independence. The American President had not taken the time to see him then. Now the United States blocked proposed re-unification elections for fear that Ho Chi Minh would emerge the winner. Instead, in the south, Americans were persuaded that they could construct a democratic state – the republic of South Vietnam – under the leadership of Ngo Dinh Diem. When Diem proved not to be – as then Vice-President Lyndon Johnson called him – the "Winston Churchill of Southeast Asia," democracy promotion became less important than defending the South against renewed efforts from the North to reunify Vietnam under communist control. The coup that overthrew Diem, coming three weeks after the assassination of John F. Kennedy in the United States, left Lyndon Johnson to decide what should be done.

Johnson opted for war. Congress gave him a "blank check" in passing the Tonkin Gulf Resolution in response to alleged North Vietnamese attacks on American naval vessels. It authorized the President to take whatever action he thought was necessary to defend American interests, together with those of its allies in the region. Following his landslide re-election in 1964, the President escalated American military involvement. Four years later, the nation's armed forces in Vietnam were, according to the newscaster Walter Cronkite, "mired in stalemate." In 1968 Johnson announced he would not run for re-election. The war ended in 1973 with the Paris Peace Accords that allowed President Richard Nixon to claim "peace with honor." Two years later, Vietnam was finally re-unified as South Vietnam capitulated to a communist invasion from the North.

In the United States the Democrats remained divided as a consequence of America's war in Southeast Asia. Some retreated from liberal internationalism. The so-called "Vietnam Syndrome" expressed their reluctance to sanction further military action overseas in support of foreign policy objectives. Others believed that American power – and indeed the President's capacity to lead – was undermined to the extent that the United States refused to exercise its military options when faced with threats in the international arena. In 1976, Jimmy Carter won the party's presidential nomination, defeating among others Senator Henry "Scoop" Jackson, who had been one of Johnson's staunchest allies in the party during the Vietnam War and who remained an advocate for a robust anti-communist foreign policy supported by military action if necessary. Some of Jackson's supporters left the Democrats and joined the Reagan administration in 1980 as neo-conservative advocates of the use of American power.

NEO-CONSERVATIVES

Following the Vietnam War, neo-conservatives became increasingly influential in the Republican party as advocates of the re-assertion of American military power in support of its foreign policy ambitions. With the collapse of the Soviet Union, these included the promotion of democratic values across the globe. In 1997, prominent neo-conservatives supported the "Project for the New American Century" which aimed "to make the case and rally support for American global leadership." Following the events of 9/11 neo-conservatives argued for military action against Afghanistan and Iraq.

Reagan referred to Vietnam as "a noble cause." Nevertheless, he remained constrained by congressional reluctance to fund American military interventionism in support of his staunchly anti-communist foreign policy, notably in South America. His administration's efforts to circumvent this restraint led to Lieutenant Oliver North's "neat idea": trading arms for hostages in the Middle East and using the proceeds to fund a proxy war against communism in Nicaragua. When North testified before the congressional committee investigating the scandal, he revealed how, while working as a military aide on the National Security Council, he had put into action "Operation Democracy." Money made from selling arms to the Khomeini regime in Iran (an activity which was illegal under US law) was deposited in secret bank accounts in Switzerland. It was then used to buy military supplies for the rebel Contras who were fighting against the communist Sandinista government in Nicaragua.

At first the President attempted to deflect criticism, but in a televised address from the Oval Office in March 1987, he was finally forced to admit that "A few months ago I told the American people I did not trade arms for hostages. My heart and my best intentions still tell me that's true, but the facts and the evidence tell me it is not." Reagan survived the "Iran-Contra" scandal, but it demonstrated the continuing tension that existed between the Executive's desire for freedom of action in conducting foreign policy and the Legislature's demand for accountability and constitutional restraint. Neo-conservative supporters blamed the "Vietnam Syndrome" and argued that it had become an obstacle to be "overcome" in order that the war's legacy did not continue to limit presidential power in the conduct of foreign affairs.

The New World Order

On November 9, 1989 the collapse of the Berlin Wall symbolized the end of the Cold War as the Soviet Union's satellites in Eastern Europe spun out of its control and its own communist regime imploded. Francis Fukuyama, a prominent neo-conservative, proclaimed the "end of history." The developments in Europe appeared to endorse Woodrow Wilson's confident faith in democracy as the culmination of civilization which would be the preferred choice of peoples across the world, if only they were permitted to shape the forms of government under which they lived. Charles Krauthammer, another neo-conservative, argued that it was a "unipolar moment" in which the United States, as the sole remaining superpower, was in an unrivalled position to exert its influence on world affairs. In these new circumstances, United States foreign policy needed to be re-focused in a world where its old ideological enemies appeared to have changed their ways.

Some tyrants remained. For President George H.W. Bush, Saddam Hussein's invasion of Kuwait in 1990 was a challenge to what he defined as the "New World Order" that was emerging after the Cold War. Acting under a United Nations mandate, the United States dominated an international coalition which ended the Iraqi dictator's expansionist ambitions in the brief air and land war of "Desert Storm." Significantly, in its immediate aftermath, Bush proclaimed that the United States had "kicked the Vietnam Syndrome once and for all" by successfully committing its military overseas. Equally revealing was his decision not to involve American forces in a protracted campaign in Iraq aimed at regime change there, instead preferring to adopt a strategy of containment to avoid any risk of "another Vietnam."

During the 1990s Americans continued to be divided whenever strategic engagement with the world was accompanied by the potential need for military action. To his critics, President Clinton's humanitarian intervention in Somalia, which ended in military embarrassment in Mogadishu, had little to do with the national interest. Yet for the President, the reason for committing American forces to a peacekeeping mission in a war-torn African nation was clear. If the United States remained on the sidelines, Clinton argued:

> our leadership in world affairs would be undermined at the very time when people are looking to America to help promote

peace and freedom in the post–Cold War world. And all around
the world, aggressors, thugs and terrorists will conclude that the
best way to get us to change our policies is to kill our people. It
would be open season on Americans.

Nevertheless, such sentiments did not lead to American intervention at the time of the tribal massacres in Rwanda. Ethnic
rivalries and religious tensions that had been suppressed during
the Cold War era of superpower rivalry in Europe presented the
United States with fresh challenges. When war broke out in the
Balkans, Clinton appeared undecided as to how America should
respond, before finally supporting NATO intervention there.
After Vietnam, Americans remained reluctant to support military
action where there was not a clear-cut threat to the nation's
security and where the success of the campaign was unpredictable. Unlike Rwanda, however, peace in Europe was a strategic
objective that called for presidential action. In March 1999,
Clinton argued that in Bosnia, "We learned that if you don't
stand up to brutality and the killing of innocent people, you
invite the people who do it to do more of it."

The President's encouragement of what Anthony Lake, his
national security adviser, called "democratic enlargement" was a
pragmatic attempt to base American foreign policy on new, post-
Cold War principles. Lake suggested that: "the successor to a
doctrine of containment must be a strategy of enlargement –
enlargement of the world's free community … We must counter
the aggression – and support the liberalization – of states hostile
to democracy." Such rhetoric harked back once more to the traditional strain of Wilsonian idealism in American foreign policy.
Yet to his Republican critics, Clinton's interventions in Somalia
and the Balkans were risky mistakes. They did little to advance
the national interest. In his 2000 presidential election campaign,
George W. Bush derided and dismissed the idea of promoting
democracy through attempts at "nation building" overseas.

Instead he argued the need for an American approach to international relations based upon "idealism without illusions," a phrase that he might have used to attract bi-partisan support since it was borrowed from his Democrat predecessor John F. Kennedy. As a candidate for the White House, Bush outlined his view that:

> An American president should work with our strong democratic allies in Europe and Asia to extend the peace. He should promote a fully democratic Western Hemisphere, bound together by free trade. He should defend America's interests in the Persian Gulf and advance peace in the Middle East, based upon a secure Israel. He must check the contagious spread of weapons of mass destruction, and the means to deliver them. He must lead toward a world that trades in freedom. And he must pursue all these goals with focus, patience and strength.

Less than nine months after he entered the White House, however, his foreign policy was irrevocably shaped by the events of September 11, 2001.

9/11 and the "war on terror"

America's response to 9/11 was predictable. For the President, the terrorist threat, like that of Cold War communism, was existential. Nations had the same choice that Harry Truman had outlined between a way of life based upon democratic values, freedom and respect for human rights or one that promoted "terror and oppression." In declaring his "war on terror," Bush argued that national security could only be preserved through taking military action. At first this would be punitive: attacking al Qaeda in its adopted homeland of Afghanistan and overthrowing the Taliban regime that had given it sanctuary. Then it would be pre-emptive: the invasion of Iraq was justified on the grounds that Saddam Hussein might have weapons of mass destruction that he, or terrorist organizations, would use in further attacks against the United States. America invaded Afghanistan with approval of the United Nations and with broad-based international support. In Iraq, after the UN failed to agree a resolution endorsing its action, it went ahead more or less unilaterally with its forces dominating the much reduced membership of a "coalition of the willing." Both military actions achieved their short-term objectives of regime change but with increasingly damaging long-term consequences for America's standing in the world. Endemic political corruption in Afghanistan and a continuing insurgency in Iraq limited the prospects for democracy taking root in either country. Domestic and international opinion increasingly questioned American strategy.

President Bush's problems compounded. No weapons of mass destruction were found in Iraq, undermining his rationale for invasion. Moreover, the aggressive expansion of presidential power in the aftermath of 9/11 was used to institute internment without trial of terrorist suspects from Afghanistan and elsewhere at Guantanamo, to allow the degradation of detainees at the Abu Ghraib prison in Iraq, to endorse practices of interrogation that amounted to torture and to permit the practice of "extraordinary rendition" of terrorist suspects to countries where the abuse of human rights was habitual rather than occasional. When the administration was discovered to have authorized surveillance of its own citizens it seemed that such actions taken in the name of national security undermined the very values that the President argued the war was necessary to protect.

Barack Obama: continuity not change

Even before he entered the White House, there was enough evidence in Barack Obama's writings, speeches and nominations to foreign policy positions in his administration to suggest that his broad perspective on the United States and its contemporary place in the world was very much in the mainstream of traditional American attitudes. His rhetoric was reminiscent of that of Woodrow Wilson. His assumption of American primacy and acceptance of the use of military power to support the national interest harked back to Theodore Roosevelt. Obama reworked the themes of progressive internationalism that had been re-echoing in Washington for over a century. As President, he appointed Hillary Clinton, another progressive internationalist, as his Secretary of State and asked Robert Gates, George W. Bush's incumbent Secretary of Defense, to stay on at the Pentagon. His worldview was outlined in *The Audacity of Hope*, in a largely anecdotal chapter: "The World beyond our Borders." Obama drew upon his childhood experience of growing up in Indonesia to suggest his cosmopolitanism. He described his more recent visits as a Senator to Iraq after the invasion and to the former Soviet Union to inspect stockpiles of weapons of mass destruction as evidence of his broadranging interest in international affairs. At the same time he confessed admiration for the achievements of Ronald Reagan during the 1980s, when Obama was coming of age politically. He wrote that he shared with the former Republican President:

> pride in our country, respect for our armed forces, a healthy appreciation for the dangers beyond our borders, an insistence that there was no easy equivalence between East and West ... And when the Berlin wall came tumbling down, I had to give the old man his due, even if I never gave him my vote.

In November 2007, the Center for Strategic and International Studies published *A Smarter More Secure America*, a report edited by Richard Armitage, who had most recently served as

Colin Powell's deputy at the State Department during George W. Bush's first administration, and Joseph Nye, a long-time advocate of the use of "soft power" – the attractive quality of America's culture, values and ideas – to help achieve its foreign policy goals. Armitage and Nye thus called upon the United States to "become a smarter power by investing once again in the global good – providing things that people and governments in all quarters of the world want but cannot attain in the absence of American leadership." This could be achieved by renewing emphasis on the importance of building alliances, promoting global development and engaging in public diplomacy, as well as through encouraging economic integration and the development of new, innovative technologies. Such ideas informed the ambitious foreign policy agenda that Obama outlined during his presidential campaign, which included his commitments to work with America's allies to take action on such issues as climate change and United Nations reform. As a candidate his unique foreign policy selling point was his early and consistent opposition to the Iraq War. Obama called it "a dumb war, a rash war, a war based not on reason but on passion, not on principle but on politics." This did not mean that as President he was opposed to taking military action to defend national security and to maintain the balance of power in international relations. In his words: "there will be times when we must ... play the role of the world's reluctant sheriff. This will not change – nor should it."

"Smart power" offered a change of style rather than substance in American foreign policy. Obama's core assumption, as he made clear in an article published in *Foreign Affairs* in June 2007, was that "the American moment is not over, but it must be seized anew." He appreciated that international alliances were essential and that the United States "must also consider using military force in circumstances beyond self-defense in order to provide for the common security that underpins global stability – to support friends, participate in stability and reconstruction operations, or confront mass atrocities." International cooperation was also necessary to prevent Iran from acquiring nuclear weapons and to persuade North Korea to abandon them, but if both remained intransigent, then Obama was adamant that he would not "take the military option off the table." Such bellicosity suggested that he wanted to avoid the perception that had clung to Jimmy Carter after the Vietnam War, that a President whose predecessors committed American forces to costly and counter-productive conflicts overseas may be reluctant to exercise a military option as America's Commander-in-Chief.

For Obama, winning hearts and minds became critical in the contemporary "war on terror." For reasons of rational self-interest, the United States, he argued:

> must invest still more in human intelligence and deploy additional trained operatives and diplomats with specialized knowledge of local cultures and languages ... We need to deepen our knowledge of the circumstances and beliefs that underpin extremism in order to combat it.

America's experience in Afghanistan and Iraq provided the impetus for a new strategic engagement with the world that Obama was optimistic could attract bi-partisan support.

In his inaugural address, therefore, Obama acknowledged the nature and the scope of the challenges facing America:

> That we are in the midst of crisis is now well understood. Our nation is at war, against a far-reaching network of violence and hatred. Our economy is badly weakened, a consequence of greed and irresponsibility on the part of some, but also our collective failure to make hard choices and prepare the nation for a new age.

Aware that the United States had lost international support as a result of the conduct of the "war on terror," the President sought to reaffirm the nation's dedication to its fundamental principles:

> as for our common defense, we reject as false the choice between our safety and our ideals. Our founding fathers, faced with perils that we can scarcely imagine, drafted a charter to assure the rule of law and the rights of man, a charter expanded by the blood of generations. Those ideals still light the world, and we will not give them up for expedience's sake.

His first foreign policy actions were symbolic. President Obama moved swiftly to revoke George W. Bush's executive orders that had limited the public release of the records of former Presidents and which sanctioned the continued use of some forms of excessive coercion in the interrogation of terrorist suspects. He announced he would close the detention camp at Guantanamo Bay – although in practice it proved difficult for the administration to gain congressional support on this issue. Detention policy practices and options were reassessed. On the day after his inauguration, Obama ordered a review of America's military strategy in Iraq and just over a month later, in a speech at Camp Lejeune in North Carolina, he announced the timetable for "a transition to full Iraqi responsibility," looking forward to "an Iraq which is sovereign, stable and self-reliant." The President announced that America's combat mission there would end by August 31, 2010. Some forces would remain to support the Iraqi government as it took over responsibility for national security, but Obama made a further commitment "to remove all US troops from Iraq by the end of 2011." The withdrawal of America's military forces was underpinned by the principles of "smart power." Obama argued the case for a "smarter, more sustainable and comprehensive approach" to the Middle East. This involved "refocusing on al Qaeda in Afghanistan and Pakistan" as well as "developing a strategy to use all elements of American power" to halt Iran's ambition to build nuclear weapons, and trying to broker "a lasting peace between Israel and the Arab world."

Prior to his North Carolina speech, Obama had approved a request to send more troops to Afghanistan. On March 27 he continued his recalibration of the "war on terror," reiterating the need for "a stronger, smarter and comprehensive strategy." This would redeploy American forces "to disrupt, dismantle and defeat Al Qaeda," both there and in Pakistan. As the military commitment to Iraq wound down, the President continued the fight against potential terrorists and the Taliban in the border region that he identified as having become "for the American people ... the most dangerous place in the world." It was "an international security challenge of the highest order" in which "the safety of people around the world is at stake." This military stimulus package to confront the deteriorating situation in Afghanistan and Pakistan was a political gamble with an unpredictable outcome. Obama's first overseas trip as President was thus focused not only on building an international consensus behind his effort to jumpstart the global economy, but also on attempting to persuade America' s NATO allies to support his new strategy in the "war on terror." His international celebrity did not make European powers less reluctant to help the American campaign. Later in 2009 the President spent several weeks deliberating before deciding to send more troops to Afghanistan, albeit with a strict time-scale for their withdrawal, in an attempt to stabilize the military situation there.

In June 2010, Obama was forced to replace General Stanley McChrystal with General David Petraeus. His initial choice as commander of coalition forces in Afghanistan, increasingly frustrated by the lack of progress there, had made disparaging remarks about the President and his administration in an interview published in *Rolling Stone* magazine. In Petraeus, Obama turned to the architect of the American "surge" in Iraq that had provided the camouflage of a temporary respite in the insurgency sufficient to allow the United States to wind down its military commitment there. Nevertheless, as Afghanistan became "Obama's war" it posed a significant threat to his political future. He risked the opening of a "credibility gap" of the kind suffered by Lyndon Johnson and George W. Bush as Commanders-in-Chief after they had committed American forces to the lengthy and unsuccessful conflicts in Vietnam and Iraq.

In December 2009, in his speech in Oslo accepting the Nobel Peace Prize, Obama observed that "the instruments of war do have a role to play in preserving the peace." They have also played a fundamental role in American foreign policy. In the nineteenth century, the expansion of the United States across the American continent was achieved initially by diplomatic negotiation – the Louisiana Purchase – and then by force of arms against Mexico. America's isolation from Europe was providential. Manifest Destiny could be pursued under the protective cover of the Monroe Doctrine. The United States claimed freedom to act in its national interests even before it became a world power.

By the beginning of the twentieth century, its territorial acquisitions, natural resources, economic enterprise and technological development allowed the United States to compete with contemporary powers in the international arena, but isolationism remained a powerful anchor. Indeed as the ability to realize foreign policy objectives became increasingly associated with military interventions overseas, isolationists saw little to recommend in such actions. Progressive internationalists like Theodore Roosevelt wanted America to carve out a role on the international stage that befitted its status as a world power. Woodrow Wilson provided the rationale: national security at home could best be preserved by fighting for democratic values abroad. That has been ever since a refrain in American presidential rhetoric, whether articulated in the context of the existential threat of communist expansion or of terrorist ambition.

As the United States has grown more powerful militarily, it has retained the feeling of insecurity and the sense of vulnerability that have been present since its creation as a democratic republic in a world dominated by imperial monarchs. In terms of ensuring national security against conventional attacks or invasion by another country, Franklin Roosevelt's famous line in his inaugural address applies to the nation's military capacity as much as it did to the contemporary domestic situation he faced. America has "nothing to fear but fear itself." But Roosevelt's successors in the White House also have had to engage with a world that faces the reality of one of his most enduring legacies. Nuclear weapons and their proliferation were abiding concerns during the Cold War, and have re-emerged as a clear and present danger in the "war on terror." The decision to retaliate in kind in response to a nuclear attack or to launch a first strike to prevent such an event happening remains the President's alone. This is a formidable responsibility and a heavy burden.

As America has assumed its role as the guarantor of world peace, its Commander-in-Chief has also had to decide when to deploy the nation's non-nuclear armed forces. Presidential wars, fought in the absence of a constitutional declaration by Congress that takes the United States into battle, have become domestically unpopular if their length becomes indeterminate and the nation can no longer tolerate their inevitable casualties. Nevertheless, the experiences of Korea, Vietnam, Afghanistan and Iraq have not diminished the propensity of Presidents to seek military solutions to political problems. When Obama observed to his audience in Oslo that he was now responsible for two wars, he was acknowledging his inheritance from his predecessor. His decision to escalate one conflict even as he extricated the United States from the other was a high risk strategy. The "idea of America" abroad meets with resistance if it is enforced at the point of a gun: a dilemma still present at the heart of American foreign policy that even "smart power" may do little to resolve.

7

Conclusion: Democracy in America

Throughout the history of its democratic republic, a crisis in national affairs focuses attention on the President of the United States. Examples of assertive presidential power – Lincoln during the Civil War or Franklin Roosevelt during the economic collapse of the 1930s and the Second World War – are tolerated only for the duration of these temporary emergencies. The checks and balances of powers between the separate institutions of the federal government and the guarantees expressed in the Bill of Rights have helped to preserve a constitutional equilibrium over time. Those Presidents who aspire to greatness may welcome crisis for the opportunities it brings them to act forcefully in the role. They may even be tempted to exaggerate the challenges they face for political effect. According to John F. Kennedy, for example, "great crises produce great men, and great deeds of courage." As President he clearly relished the opportunity of testing himself at a time when Cold War tensions were at their height. In his inaugural address, he talked of his generation's historic role "of defending freedom in its hour of maximum danger." Shortly afterwards, in his first State of the Union address, Kennedy borrowed the language of Lincoln in warning that "before my term has ended, we shall have to test anew whether a nation organized and governed such as ours can endure." Such dramatic rhetoric emphasized the contemporary confrontations that he argued faced the nation and its new President. The journalist Henry Fairlie captured the mood when he observed that throughout Kennedy's presidency, the United States "lived in an atmosphere of perpetual crisis and recurring crises ... policy was subjected to crisis, and crisis was used in turn to stimulate the response of the people ... So they lived for a thousand days in expectation of danger, and of rescue from it." Indeed, Kennedy's time in the White House would be defined by the Cuban Missile Crisis which brought the United States and the Soviet Union to the brink of nuclear war.

However, a Chief Executive's interpretation of how to exercise the constitutional powers of the office at a time of crisis can also fatally undermine the legitimacy of presidential leadership. Richard Nixon wrote of his belief that during his administration the United States was "torn apart in an ideological way by the war in Vietnam, as much as the Civil War tore apart the nation when Lincoln was president." Politically beleaguered, he looked to Lincoln for help. He pointed out that it was the first Republican President who had said that "actions which otherwise would be unconstitutional, could become lawful if undertaken for the purpose of preserving the Constitution and the Nation." For Nixon that meant that "there have been – and will be in the future – circumstances in which presidents may lawfully authorize actions in the interests of the security of this country, which if undertaken by other persons, even by the president under different circumstances, would be illegal." Or more succinctly, as he said during his televised interviews with David Frost, "if the President does it, that means it's not illegal." That interpretation of the Constitution proved to be so controversial that Nixon had by then been forced to resign the presidency before he was impeached by Congress. In times of national crisis, the modern Chief Executive walks a tightrope across the political chasm that separates what is within and what is beyond the bounds of the President's constitutional powers.

Challenges abroad

Even before his inauguration, Barack Obama was being compared in flattering terms to two of those judged to be among his
most illustrious predecessors, both of whom had expanded the
sphere of presidential power during their time in the White
House. On *Time* magazine's front cover, Obama was portrayed as
a latter day Franklin Roosevelt, who had also taken office at a
time of economic depression and who had re-ignited the
American people's confidence in their country. Elsewhere, he
appeared as another Abraham Lincoln who had come to
Washington from Illinois and who had steered the United States
through the Civil War. However, both Lincoln and Roosevelt
had entered the White House in succession to Presidents – James
Buchanan and Herbert Hoover – who had been unable to assert
effective presidential leadership in the face of crisis. In contrast, to
many of his critics, George W. Bush, Obama's predecessor, had
used executive power aggressively and ultimately to damaging
effect on the institution itself. They argued that his "war on
terror" had put national security concerns before the protection
of individual rights and civil liberties. The widespread international sympathy for the United States in the immediate aftermath of 9/11 had evaporated following the invasion of Iraq.
Obama inherited the challenges of crisis with limited room for
political maneuver.

George W. Bush left the White House with his reputation in
tatters. The wars he had started in Afghanistan and Iraq were still
raging, the memories of his handling of the aftermath of
Hurricane Katrina, which in 2005 destroyed New Orleans and
damaged much of the Gulf Coast, still lingered and the global
banking system was drowning under a tsunami of toxic debt. In
addition he had presided over financial scandals, the beginning of
the worst economic recession since the 1930s, and the creation
of a federal budget deficit that had assumed stratospheric lift-off

even before the bail-outs to the banks made it astronomical. His administration, under the watchful eye of Vice-President Dick Cheney, had expanded executive power after the events of 9/11. This created a set of unique circumstances for his successor: faced with crises that in the past might have allowed presidential authority to be used with greater latitude, Barack Obama entered the White House at a time when the Executive had been accused of re-establishing the much maligned "imperial presidency" that had imploded in the scandal of Watergate.

Rahm Emanuel, Obama's chief of staff, observed in November 2008: "you never want to let a serious crisis go to waste." As the aftershocks of the banking collapse were felt throughout the economy, the new administration saw the opportunity to bring about fundamental changes in America's political landscape through addressing neglected problems: the provision of health-care, high levels of energy consumption and dependence upon oil, the distribution of wealth through the tax system, standards of education and the need for regulation of the financial sector. Obama, who had at one time taught constitutional law at the University of Chicago, understood that leadership could be exer-cised within the framework of separated institutions sharing powers rather than through an attempt to short-circuit the polit-ical system. During his first months in the White House, the President lived up to the phrase coined by the media to describe his approach to the challenges he faced. "No drama Obama" adopted a managerial approach to the economic crisis in which the President's relationship with Congress became key to his agenda of change. Helped by temporary, if not always reliable, Democrat majorities in the House of Representatives and the Senate, when his appeals to bi-partisanship proved futile, the President was still able to achieve legislative success, most signifi-cantly on the signature issue of his campaign: healthcare reform.

This pragmatic and low-key approach to presidential leader-ship had much to do with the necessary recalibration of the initial expectations surrounding his election and inauguration as Obama crossed the road from the campaign trail to the White House. Yet the administration's reaction to events was still judged in the light of the demand for presidential action in the face of perceived crisis. Initially criticized for being slow to realize the catastrophic impact of what became America's worst environmental disaster when the BP oil-rig "Deepwater Horizon" exploded in the Gulf of Mexico in April 2010, Obama scrambled to recover from accusations that the oil washing up on America's shores represented his Hurricane Katrina. Although, as he said, he could not "dive down there and plug the hole," once he had regained some of the political initiative in dealing with the issue, the President was nevertheless able to use the incident as a way of advancing his political agenda: another example of using crisis as a potential catalyst for change. In his first address from the Oval Office, therefore, Obama argued that the disaster demonstrated that the United States had to break its reliance on oil as a principle source for its high levels of energy consumption. It was another example of a neglected problem:

> for decades, we have known the days of cheap and easily accessible oil were numbered. For decades, we've talked and talked about the need to end America's century-long addiction to fossil fuels. And for decades, we have failed to act with the sense of urgency that this challenge require … The consequences of our inaction are now in plain sight … The tragedy unfolding on our coast is the most painful and powerful reminder yet that the time to embrace a clean energy future is now. Now is the moment for this generation to embark on a national mission to unleash America's innovation and seize control of our own destiny.

In pressing the case for breaking America's dependency upon oil – much of it imported from politically volatile areas such as the Middle East – Obama connected the rhetoric of the past with his vision of America's future. The language of "mission" and "destiny" associated the search for alternative energy sources with the pioneering spirit which had underpinned the expansion of Jefferson's "Empire for Liberty" during the nineteenth century. The "bully pulpit" of the presidency remains a powerful tool of persuasion. However, at the same time, Obama's agenda of change also created a political backlash that provided a stark contrast to the initial enthusiasm surrounding his election. The emergence of the Tea Party movement as a political force in the United States demonstrates that the President does not have a monopoly on the use of historical imagery to dramatize contemporary issues. The events in Boston Harbor in 1773 remain a symbol of American defiance against authority. Opposed to elements of Obama's "stimulus package," healthcare reform and any tax increases, the Tea Party movement described itself as a "community committed to standing together, shoulder to shoulder, to protect our country and the Constitution upon which we were founded." The potential of its grass roots energy was soon appreciated among those Republicans who had experienced the party's comprehensive rejection at the polls during the 2008 election, not least the defeated Vice-Presidential candidate, Sarah Palin.

Nevertheless, on November 5, 2008, the night that he won the marathon race for the presidency, in his speech at Grant Park, Chicago, Obama attempted to sum up the meaning of his victory:

> If there is anyone out there who still doubts that America is a place where all things are possible; who still wonders if the dream of our founders is alive in our time; who still questions the power of our democracy, tonight is your answer … It's the answer that led those who have been told for so long by so many to be cynical, and fearful, and doubtful of what we can

achieve to put their hands on the arc of history and bend it once more toward the hope of a better day.

His ability to win the White House suggested that American society is becoming more inclusive than it has been in the past, but only when more of his successors do not routinely resemble the faces on the nation's banknotes will his extraordinary achievement become mundane. In 1776 and again in 1787, the arc of American history was bent first toward the prospect of independence and then toward the creation of the United States as a federal republic. More than two centuries later, that vision still inspires the future of democracy in America.

Further reading

Introduction

The BBC's foreign correspondent in Washington DC, Matt Frei, gives useful insights into aspects of the nation's political culture in *Only in America* (Harper Perennial, 2009). A standard historical survey is Hugh Brogan's *The Penguin History of the United States of America* (Penguin, 2001). Barack Obama, *Dreams from My Father: A Story of Race and Inheritance* (Canongate Books, 2008), can be read both as autobiography and as a deeper meditation on issues of race and identity in contemporary American society.

Chapter 1

In *Inventing America: Jefferson's Declaration of Independence* (Mariner Books, 2002), Garry Wills interprets the political thought that underpins this critical document of the founding period. John Jay, Alexander Hamilton and James Madison wrote the operating manual of the Constitution in a series of articles just after it was agreed at the Philadelphia Convention in 1787. Collected and published in book form, it has ever since remained in print. *The Federalist Papers* (Oxford University Press, 2008) is a recent edition. Alexis de Tocqueville's *Democracy in America* (Wordsworth Editions, 1998) is the classic analysis of the political culture of the United States in the nineteenth century. His later observations on American politics have recently been collected and published in Aurelian Craiutu and Jeremy Jennings (eds.), *Tocqueville on*

America after 1840: Letters and Other Writings (Cambridge University Press, 2009).

Chapter 2

Richard Neustadt, *Presidential Power and the Modern Presidents: The Politics of Leadership from Roosevelt to Reagan* (The Free Press, 1991), examines how Presidents can operate effectively within the American political system. In *The Imperial Presidency* (Mariner Books, 2004), Arthur Schlesinger Jr. provides an analysis of the historical developments which have encouraged some Chief Executives to ignore the constitutional restraints on their actions. Donald A. Ritchie's *The US Congress: A Very Short Introduction* (OUP USA, 2010) is no less useful for being concise. *The Oxford Guide to Supreme Court Decisions* (OUP USA, 2009), edited by Kermit Hall and James Ely, contains historical and biographical material about the court, together with a survey of the most significant cases it has decided.

Chapter 3

Larry Sabato and Howard Ernst have compiled an *Encyclopedia of American Political Parties and Elections* (Checkmark Books, 2007). The collection of essays in Jeffrey Stonecash (ed.), *New Directions in American Political Parties* (Routledge, 2010), provides insights into how parties are responding to changes in American society. In *Campaigns and Elections American Style* (Westview Press, 2008), the editors, James Thurber and Candice Nelson, bring together political scientists and practitioners to discuss different aspects of electoral and campaign politics.

Chapter 4

In Iwan Morgan and Philip Davies (eds.), *The Federal Nation: Perspectives on American Federalism* (Palgrave Macmillan, 2009), contributors consider the variety of issues surrounding contemporary federal politics in the United States. Darrell Kozlowski and Jennifer Weber's work, *Federalism* (Chelsea House Publishers, 2010) examines the development of the concept in American political life. The second edition of Michael Reagan and John Sanzone's book, *The New Federalism* (OUP USA, 1981), was published in the year that the President who shared the name of one of the authors entered the White House, and outlines some of the themes that informed Ronald Reagan's approach to the subject.

Chapter 5

Frank Lambert, *Religion in American Politics: A Short History* (Princeton University Press, 2008), is a good introduction to this important topic. So too is Mark Hulsether's *Religion, Culture and Politics in the Twentieth Century United States* (Columbia University Press, 2007). In *Under God: Religion and American Politics* (Simon and Schuster, 1991), Garry Wills examines the ways in which religion and politics have intersected and includes an analysis of the impact of Darwin's thought upon the religious community in the United States.

Chapter 6

A standard text is Bruce Jentleson, *American Foreign Policy: The Dynamics of Choice in the 21st Century* (W.W. Norton, 2010). Timothy Lynch and Robert Singh argue that the events of 9/11 did little to change America's perspectives on the wider world in *After Bush: The Case for Continuity in American Foreign Policy* (Cambridge University Press, 2008). The latest in Bob Woodward's series of investigative books, begun during George W. Bush's presidency, examining presidential decision making in committing American military forces overseas, is *Obama's Wars: The Inside Story* (Simon and Schuster, 2010).

Chapter 7

Gillian Peele et al. (eds.), *Developments in American Politics 6* (Palgrave Macmillan, 2010) surveys the framework of contemporary American government and discusses policy issues in the context of the Obama administration. Cal Jillson's *American Government: Political Development and Institutional Change* (Routledge, 2011) is the sixth edition of a lively and informative work. Some of the themes that define American political culture which are outlined in this guide are also discussed in Jon Roper, *The Contours of American Politics* (Polity, 2002).

Index